Addictions and Trauma Recovery

Addictions and Trauma Recovery

Healing the Mind, Body, and Spirit

Dusty Miller
Laurie Guidry

W·W·NORTON

NEW YORK · LONDON

Copyright © 2001 by Dusty Miller and Laurie Guidry

For information about permission to reproduce
selections from this book, write to
Permissions, W. W. Norton & Company, Inc.,
500 Fifth Avenue, New York, NY 10110

Composition and book design by Ecomlinks, Inc.
Manufacturing by Hamilton Printing
Production Manager: Leeann Graham

Library of Congress Cataloging-in-Publication Data
Miller, Dusty, 1944-
    Addictions and trauma recovery: healing the mind, body, and spirit/Dusty Miller,
    Laurie Guidry.
        p.   cm.
    "A Norton professional book."
    Includes bibliographical references and index.
ISBN 978-0-3937-0368-9
    1. Women—Mental health. 2. Women—Counseling of. 3. Psychic trauma. 4.
Self-destructive behavior. I. Guidry, Laurie. II. Title.

RC451.4.W6 M567 2001
616.89—dc21   2001030353

W. W. Norton & Company, Inc., 500 Fifth Avenue, New York, NY 10110
www.wwnorton.com
W. W. Norton & Company, Ltd., Castle House, 75/76 Wells Street, London W1T 3QT
                    4 5 6 7 8 9 0

Contents

Part IV: The Inner Circle

Acknowledgments

We want to thank those who made this project possible. The women who have participated in our ATRIUM groups have helped us create this model and this manual: They have been trusting and generous teachers. Thanks to pioneers Paki Wieland, Elaine Campbell, Susan Quigley, and Helen Daly who first guided Dusty Miller's earlier model into a group format and revitalized the work. Thanks also to Pat Bradway who offered valuable insights, interventions, and editing assistance in the pilot stage of the manual and to Jane Linsley who contributed thoughtful and useful additions to the work.

This manual was generously supported by Rene Anderson and the Western Massachusetts Training Consortium: We are grateful to Rene for her vision. Thanks also to Susan Salasin at SAMHSA for her courageous leadership.

Very special thanks go to Kathy Kennedy at the Consortium who rescued us from cyber nightmares repeatedly!

We also wish to thank Deborah Malmud and Christine Habermaas at Norton for their intelligent and gracious editorial support.

Without the infinite patience, support, and nurturance of our friends and loved ones—especially Paki Wieland and Suellynn Stark—we would not be able to do the work we do, including the writing of this book; we dedicate this to you with deep gratitude. A special dedication is also made in memory of Jen S. and Bea S.—two brave women who taught invaluable lessons about the struggle to be human.

Finally, we want to acknowledge our gratitude for the work we are privileged to do and the gift of working together.

Addictions and Trauma Recovery

Part I
Introduction
to the ATRIUM Model

The ATRIUM Model

The **"Addiction and Trauma Recovery Integration Model"** (ATRIUM) has been developed for survivors and their allies, as well as for group leaders. It is designed for use by groups as well as individual consumers and their counselors/therapists and peer support network. The ATRIUM protocol is based on Dusty Miller's *Trauma Reenactment Model*, published in 1994, an assessment and recovery model for people with trauma-related mental health and addiction challenges. ATRIUM is intended for the following:

- people with substance abuse and other addictive behaviors
- people who addictively engage in harmful relationships
- people who self-injure
- people with serious psychiatric diagnoses
- people who are survivors of sexual and physical abuse
- people who enact violence and abuse against others

Trauma impacts the survivor at three levels: the body, the mind, and the spirit. The ATRIUM model is a process designed to assess and intervene at all three of those levels. This model is unique in its practical approach to healing the body and the spirit as well as the mind.

The ATRIUM model is the product of consumer/survivor experience as well as professional expertise. The authors' personal knowledge of the mental health system and addiction recovery serves as a foundation for the model, so that the model speaks with the voice of personal experience as well as professional knowledge. The authors hope that this manual will help both consumers and professionals find a much-needed bridge between addiction recovery and trauma-based mental health recovery, using the strength and wisdom of both professional and peer healing resources.

A Personal Account of "Addiction vs. Trauma" Treatment Lapses

I (DM) know from my experience as a client as well as from my professional vantage point that recovery has been difficult for women and men with the co-occurring challenges of addiction and trauma-based mental health problems. My own experiences as an alcoholic and trauma survivor serve as classic illustrations of the dilemmas faced by those struggling with the legacy of trauma and the horrors of addiction. Although my drinking and drugging behavior was outside of the most liberal parameters of "social use"—even for the standards of the '60s and '70s—I entered the helping system through the mental health door. I look back on my college career in the era of the civil rights movement and anti-war protests and wonder what blindfolded the mental health professionals I encountered. I was frequently engaged in black-out drinking, was hospitalized after one drinking episode (that resulted in an altercation and injury), and left school during my senior year for a period of months, jeopardizing my graduation plans. No one seemed to think there was anything remarkable about my behavior, despite my efforts to seek help from teachers, clergy, and the college counseling center where I disclosed an incestuous relationship with my father and my extreme drinking habit.

By the beginning of the '70s my relationship with alcohol and drugs worsened. During the following ten years, I was frequently heavily medicated and viewed as a good candidate for psychotropic medication despite my open preference for self-medication via alcohol and street drugs. (As the drummer in a women's rock band, I flaunted my substance use as a necessary part of my image.)

I continued to seek help from mental health professionals. My psychotherapist often talked with me for hours on the phone at night despite my obviously intoxicated condition. I was periodically hospitalized for self-destructive behavior (induced by substance abuse and traumatic memories), yet no one suggested a substance abuse treatment program or explored my history of chronic childhood sexual and physical abuse.

In 1979 a psychologist at a private psychiatric hospital where I was residing on a locked psychiatric ward invited me to move downstairs to the alcohol treatment unit. Shortly before this, I had found myself locked up in a state mental hospital on a ward for violent women. I had very little memory of how I had gotten there, and I was terrified. I was ready to admit that I had a problem with alcohol. While this was an important turning point in my recovery, there was still no treatment program available to me that helped me link my substance abuse with my childhood abuse.

My story illustrates how ill-informed both the substance abuse and the mental health fields were when it came to diagnosing and treating the complex interaction of trauma and addictions. It was not unusual for someone like me to be medicated and hospitalized for a psychiatric condition. (If I had been poor or nonwhite, the same behaviors would probably have landed me in prison instead of the hospital). It was not unusual that both my addictive behaviors and my incest history were overlooked. What is frightening is that the helping professions haven't progressed very much as we've moved into the twenty-first century.

A Brief Description of the Model

Providing a blend of psychoeducational, process, and expressive activities, the 12-week ATRIUM model is structured to address key issues linked to trauma and addiction experiences, such as anxiety, sexuality/touch, self-harm, depression, anger, physical complaints and ailments, sleep difficulty, relationship challenges, and spiritual disconnection. Information is provided on *the body*'s response to traumatic stress along with what is known about the multifarious effects of trauma on *the mind* and *the spirit*. The model also introduces participants to new ways of thinking about self-care, self-soothing (the relaxation response and mindfulness training), and self-expression (the expressive component).

■ Pervasive Interpersonal Violence

Interpersonal violence impacts men, women, and children throughout the world.[*] Many women in the United States suffer the effects of interpersonal violence, including both childhood and adult-onset abuse and neglect. (Interpersonal violence is defined here as physical and sexual assault: rape, incest, battering, and murder.) These women—and the service systems working with them—are often overwhelmed by the mental health and addiction problems resulting from interpersonal trauma and abuse. The literature on mental health issues and addiction supports the need for a comprehensive treatment approach that emphasizes building a support community for women living with the trauma of interpersonal violence, while at the same time addressing the role of trauma at the root of addictions and related mental health problems and offering new coping strategies for daily life.

---

[*]Although ATRIUM has been used to help male victims and perpetrators of violence, this book is primarily focused on healing for girls and women. For this reason, female pronouns will be used throughout the book when referring to survivors.

Interpersonal violence against women and their children is so prevalent in American society that it is described as "endemic" (Browne & Bassuk, 1997). Research collected from multiple disciplines indicates that these events are so common for women, regardless of cultural affiliation and socioeconomic class, that they have become a "normative" part of female life in the United States today. General population studies have found that 10 to 12 percent of women have been sexually abused during childhood and 13 to 17 percent of women were physically abused as children (American Medical Association (AMA), 1992; Policy Research, Inc., 1994). Further, during the period from 1988 to 1993, nearly four million women who were married or living with a male partner were physically abused. Two million women were raped. According to the Federal Bureau of Investigation's *Uniform Crime Statistics* (1992), more than one-quarter of murdered women are killed by their current or former partners. Women who are victims of violence usually experience this as violence committed by intimates. Therefore, perpetration is rarely a single event.

The Connection Between Violence and Mental Health Symptoms and Addiction

Studies show that approximately 50–70 percent of women hospitalized for psychiatric reasons (Carmen, 1995), 70 percent of those seen in emergency rooms (Briere & Zaidi, 1989), and between 40–60 percent of those seen as psychiatric outpatients report having experienced physical or sexual abuse (Briere & Runtz, 1988; Muenzenmaier, Meyer, Struening, & Ferber, 1993). Researchers have noted that women who experience physical and/or sexual abuse as children are at increased risk for the following mental health problems: depression (Herman, 1992a, 1992b; Mirowsky & Ross, 1995; Muenzenmaier et al., 1993; Rose, Peabody, & Stratigeas, 1991); posttraumatic stress reactions (Albach & Everaerd, 1992; Doob, 1992; Haswell & Graham, 1996); suicidal ideation and attempts (Briere, 1988; Carmen, 1995; Herman, 1992a; Miller, 1994, 1996); and poor self-esteem (Brayden, 1995; Glover, Janikowski, & Benshoff, 1996; Young, 1992).

More than 70 percent of women with drug or alcohol abuse problems were victims of violence, such as domestic assault by adult partners, rape, and incest (Roberts, 1998). Researchers note that women with histories of sexual and physical abuse are at risk for addictions, including: substance use/abuse (Diamond, 2000; Glover et al., 1996; Harris, 1994; Miller, 1990, 1991, 1992, 1994, 1996; Miller, Guidry, & Daly, 1999; Zlotnick, Shea, Recupero, Bidadi, Pearlstein, & Brown, 1997); eating disorders (Herman, 1992b; Janes, 1994; Miller, 1994, 1996, 1999; Young, 1992); and self-inflicted injury (Dallam, 1997; Haswell & Graham, 1996; Janes, 1994; Miller, 1990, 1994, 1996, 1999; Shapiro & Dominiak, 1992).

Women with current substance abuse problems are estimated to have a 30–59 percent rate of PTSD (Najavits, Weiss, Shaw, & Muenz, 1998); the same population shows a much higher rate of PTSD compared to men with similar substance abuse diagnoses (Brown, Huba, & Melchlor, 1995). This vulnerable group is also at high risk for adult sexual assault, domestic violence, and HIV infection.

Addictions, mental health distress, and trauma seem to form a toxic feedback loop: The mental health symptoms caused by trauma-related distress continuously stimulate the addiction compulsion. The use of substances may have seemed to be the only way the trauma survivor could self-medicate against the pain, anxiety, rage, fear, and attendant somatic distress created by overwhelming traumatic experiences (Jennings, 1997; Miller, 1994, 1996; Prescott, 1998).

Interpersonal Violence and Self-Injury

Various experts on trauma have noted the connection between self-harmful behavior and a history of sexual abuse, physical abuse, or severe neglect (Diamond, 2000; Herman, 1992b; Miller, 1994, 1996; Pearlman & Saakvitne, 1995; Shapiro & Dominiak, 1992). Many studies correlating severe childhood abuse with self-destructive behavior (Conterio & Lader, 1999; Landecker, 1992; Miller, 1994, 1996; Saakvitne, Gamble, Pearlman, & Tabor-Lev, 2000) view self-harmful or self-sabotaging behavior as the victim's way of punishing her own body because she feels responsible for or guilty about the childhood abuse. Others say that self-injury and self-sabotage are attempts to control rage, feelings of emptiness, anxiety, shame, or numbness (Herman, Perry, & van der Kolk, 1985). Some women say they are self-harmful so that they can be the ones in control of their own bodies and that self-harm is the only way they can find to tell the story of their past trauma (Miller, 1994, 1996).

One way in which women and girls may experience a reenactment of their past abuse is expressed in a pattern of participation in abusive relationships. While it is critical to emphasize that *women are not responsible or accountable for violence perpetrated against them,* there is often a connection between childhood abuse and adult relationships that are characterized by abusive dynamics. For some women, it seems impossible to escape from violent relationships because of poverty, terrorism, or the fear of losing their children or life.

There are other women who might be able to escape if they were not caught in patterns of reenacting the power and control dynamics of their childhood. The woman may seem to allow herself to be victimized as she was in childhood, unable to act in a self-protective way and thus reenacting the dynamics of not being protected in childhood. The abusive relationship may even have a certain feeling of safety, or at least inevitability, if this is how she internalized relationships as a child.

Many of the symptoms and behaviors associated with childhood abuse, such as poor self-esteem, suicidality, lack of impulse control, poor affect control and substance use, all place women at greater risk for re-victimization (Briere, 1988; Browne & Finkelhor, 1986; Muenzenmaier et al., 1993; Salasin, 1986). Current research refers to the co-occurrence of trauma, addiction, and mental health diagnoses in populations of women who also experience the cycles of terror, poverty, and shame induced by living in currently violent situations (Alexander & Muenzenmaier, 1998; Najavits, Weiss, & Liese, 1996; Walker, Gelfand, Katon, Koss, Von Korff, Bernstein, & Russo, 1999; Warshaw, 1995). Women who were abused as children are at increased risk of rape and domestic violence as adults (Alexander & Muenzenmaier, 1998; Walker et al., 1999); between 70–80 percent of women who experience domestic violence have also survived physical and/or sexual abuse during childhood (Manley, 1999).

Prevalence of Trauma and Somatic Pain and Illness

From the late nineteenth century to the present there have been many ways to understand how traumatic events translate into physical complaints. Antiquated notions of hysteria linked early "imagined" trauma to a broad range of mysterious physical manifestations that led to the identification of conversion disorders. More recently, Krystal (1988) theorized that unintegrated experiences of trauma can result in trauma survivors misinterpreting emotional responses as body-based illnesses. Contemporary empirical research by Pribor, Yutzy, Dean, and Wetzel (1993), in a field trial study for the development of the *DSM-IV* diagnostic categories, indicates that perhaps as many as 90 percent of those suffering from Somatization Disorders have histories of early trauma.

There are ongoing efforts in the investigation of the more "literal" relationship between early trauma and the subsequent development of medical illnesses as well (Green, Epstein, Krupnick, & Rowland, 1997; Schnurr, 1996). For instance, a variety of medical problems identified among women including irritable bowel syndrome and chronic pelvic pain, have been linked to early histories of childhood abuse (Walker, Katon, Roy-Byrne, Jemelka, & Russo, 1993). Increasingly, the complex relationship between early childhood abuse and the onset of physical illness is being examined and a new understanding is being cultivated.

■ History of Treatment

Whether the treatment of choice is to focus primarily on current trauma-induced behaviors or to treat the trauma through the uncovering of traumatic memories, it is common knowledge among medical and mental health professionals that survivors continue to suffer devastating symptoms and relational impasses.

In order to understand both previous treatment failures as well as the theory and practice of our approach, we think it is important to first understand the complex history of treatment and recovery in these types of cases.

Keeping It Simple: Addiction Treatment

The addiction recovery community has generally been suspicious of all treatment interventions straying from a clear and simple focus on addictive behaviors and their cognitive underpinnings. This single-minded attention to the cognitive-behavioral foundations of alcohol and drug abuse and/or eating disorders makes sense. It has been repeatedly argued that people who are struggling with addictions need to stop their addictive behavior before they are able to work on any of the underlying issues that attend the addiction. It is common sense to begin the process of recovery from drug, alcohol, or food addiction by admitting, as the first step of Alcoholics Anonymous clearly states, that one is powerless over the addiction and because of it, life has become unmanageable. Without a commitment to sobriety (abstinence from the addictive behavior), it is very difficult for anyone to begin the work of creating new patterns of thinking, behaviors, relationships, and ways of living.

Whether the addict begins his or her sobriety in a residential addiction program or through participation in daily 12-step meetings, the central goal is to stay abstinent from the primary addiction and other related addictive behaviors. It is very difficult to get clean and sober and even more difficult to continue a program of abstinence. The wisdom of the addiction treatment community suggests that by "keeping it simple," getting through "one day at a time," and going to meetings where the primary focus is on staying sober, the addict will begin to feel healthier and more able to begin the lifelong task of creating a sane life. Thus the "common sense" approach of most addiction counselors would lead them to ask why anyone in a helping role would undermine the addict's abstinence by offering to examine the underlying, painful trauma issues that might so readily trigger a relapse.

Unfortunately, for many who suffer the dual challenge of addiction and trauma-based mental health problems it may seem impossible to remain abstinent because of trauma-based physiological responses, emotions, thoughts, and relationship patterns. This trauma-related distress continuously stimulates the addiction compulsion. The use of substances may have been the best or only way the trauma survivor found to self-medicate against the pain, anxiety, rage, fear, and attendant bodily states created by overwhelming traumatic experiences.

Treatment Paradoxes in Working with Trauma-Related Addictions

For those who want to help the addicted trauma survivor, and for the women and men struggling with the co-occurring disorder, there are several treatment paradoxes to consider.

1. How can the addict give up the addictive behavior in order to address the underlying trauma issues if it is the trauma issues that create the compulsion to self-medicate?

2. What person would choose to give up something that eases chronic emotional and physical pain, and then engage in therapy that stimulates that pain without recourse to relief via self-medication?

3. How does the trauma survivor take the first step of recovery and admit powerlessness over the addiction when the addiction seems to be the only "power" he or she has to fight the pervasive internal distress created by trauma experiences?

Added to these paradoxical challenges is the central paradox of the 12-step programs—admitting powerlessness in order to combat the powerlessness of being a victim in the battle to control the addiction: *As an addict, as long as I struggle to control my addiction, I am rendered powerless because it is the nature of the addiction to control my life. When I surrender control of the addiction, admitting finally that I am indeed powerless, I will for the first time experience some control in my daily life.* This cognitive puzzle is difficult enough for any addict to comprehend, but for someone who has been victimized through the loss of control childhood trauma entails, this can be extremely frightening or counterintuitive.

Many mental health professionals are unable to help the addicted trauma survivor because of these issues surrounding abstinence and the surrender to powerlessness. Conversely, many who are engaged in the addiction recovery field, either as professional helpers or as recovering addicts, are equally unable to work with the complexities presented by persons with this particular configuration of co-occurring disorders. Addiction-based helpers may seem to be impatient with the trauma survivor's reluctance to give up the practice of self-medication, and they may not understand the survivor's terror of admitting powerlessness as the first step to recovery.

The Roots of Mistrust

One of the major obstacles to integrating addiction treatment with trauma-focused mental health treatment has been the mistrust between the worlds of addiction recovery and psychotherapy.

Those who have chosen to concentrate on addressing addictions have been suspicious of mental health professionals, often for good reason. Frequently, people struggling with addiction have had the experience of the addiction being overlooked or minimized, as in my case. Or the addict has been rejected from psychotherapy treatment, viewed as a poor candidate—not "high functioning" enough for this more verbal, insightful format for healing.

Another belief which has kept the two domains separate is that concentrating on painful childhood memories—or even current sources of emotional pain—is an excuse used to keep the alcoholic or addict from simply accepting his or her addiction as a disease for which there is no cure. "Don't drink and go to meetings" is the simple prescription—psychotherapy is seen as a dangerous detour from the reality of accepting the intractable nature of one's addiction and learning to meet life's challenges without self-medication.

Perhaps the biggest obstacle to the recovery movement's partnership with the mental health system has been the latter's liberal dispensation of prescription drugs. Why would an addict give up the bottle or the needle, only to substitute it with drugs supplied by the psychiatrist or M.D.? What could the mental health system's "drug-pushing" offer someone who could, in 12-step addiction recovery, learn a whole new way of life and become part of a worldwide, non-hierarchical community of other sober people?

From the other side of the fence, the academically trained mental health professional has historically viewed the addiction counselor with condescension. Addiction treatment is often not included in graduate training for masters and doctoral level degrees; it has been viewed as simplistic, strictly behavioral, and lacking in the complexities of the more cognitive or psychodynamically based psychotherapy models.

To date, when we have provided trainings for mental health professionals, there is a pervasive and seemingly unabashed lack of knowledge about addiction. Many mental health professionals have never attended an AA meeting or any other 12-step meeting. Many professionals have inadequate knowledge of the effects of the various drugs or other addictive behaviors their clients struggle with.

Instead of trying to explore the interconnections between addictions and psychological conditions, the mental health system has referred clients to addiction treatment facilities in order to avoid dealing with the challenge of relapse. Generally, most practitioners simply refuse psychotherapy to anyone who is drinking or taking drugs addictively. Clients with eating disorders may be accepted as good candidates for psychotherapy, but they too are referred out—usually for medical attention—as soon as the food addiction becomes dangerous (i.e., serious cases of anorexia or obesity).

Where Is Trauma Treatment Located?

Until recently, most people in the mental health system who had trauma histories suffered the same fate as people with addictions: They were likely to have their primary source of distress ignored, minimized, or denied.

Today, when someone identifies him or herself as seeking help because of childhood sexual abuse, physical abuse, or adult-onset sexual assault, he or she will very likely be routed into the mental health system. Diagnoses like posttraumatic stress disorder (PTSD), depression, anxiety disorder, or any of the personality disorders, will be applied more often than an addiction diagnosis.

The treatments offered to people with childhood trauma, or adult interpersonal violence as the primary problem vary from provider to provider. Since the mid- or late '80s when trauma finally became acknowledged as a pervasive problem with serious mental health consequences, ideas about preferred treatment modalities have changed quickly and radically. At first, it was generally believed that talking about traumatic past events in an accepting and supportive relationship was the most effective approach to trauma treatment. Reexperiencing the trauma was encouraged so that accountability could be correctly located with the perpetrator of the abuse, and powerful emotions that might have been previously repressed could be expressed in a safe reparative relationship with a therapist or counselor. At this time, there was also the rapid development of a backlash movement that tended to blame both the victim and his or her counselor, insisting that most memories of childhood trauma were not accurate and were, in fact, falsely "planted" by therapists who made false assumptions about the reality of the abuse and manipulated their unwitting clients. A more recent trend is cognitive-behavioral models that focus more on teaching the survivor how to cope with the symptoms of trauma rather than working on uncovering old memories or encouraging the expression of the intense emotions connected to the trauma.

Controversy continues as to whether it is helpful or not for someone to recall buried memories of abuse. Some providers believe that unnecessary distress can be caused by forcing the mind to recall distressing memories instead of respecting the mind's innate capacity to protect itself. This position is not the same as those who doubt that the traumatic events occurred; instead, the premise is that some trauma must have occurred, thus causing the person to have both the shadowy images or recollections suggesting trauma and the predictable symptoms generally resulting from trauma experience.

When trauma is coupled with addiction, treatment options become confusing. The safe supportive therapy relationship where the survivor can rework the story of the trauma, complete with intensely distressing emotional discharge, is generally not useful when applied to someone with entrenched addictions. Such an approach is likely to escalate the use of the addiction as the survivor attempts to self-medicate against the emotional pain stirred up by uncovering the memories of trauma. The more "here and now" cognitive approach is certainly a safer route when dealing with both trauma and addictions, but if the therapy doesn't incorporate an understanding of the interrelated addiction and the trauma, one cluster of symptoms is likely to simply convert to another set of similar symptoms. The basic patterns of the relationship—the attachment and disconnection patterns so central to the struggles of trauma survivors—remain hidden. When this happens, the ongoing loneliness and pain of the survivor continues to fuel his or her need to turn to the comfort of the addiction.

Co-occurring Disorders: Treatment for Trauma, Addictions, and Mental Health Symptoms

Recent literature states that there is still no effective treatment for women with co-occurring PTSD and substance abuse disorders (Najavits et al., 1998). Yet research also indicates that women with this particular diagnostic combination are clearly in great need of accessible, empirically validated treatment.

When mental health symptoms related to childhood trauma co-occur with addictions, the professional helping system is liable to respond with a fragmented and often unsuccessful approach. When addiction counselors find themselves working at cross purposes with mental health providers, the addiction counselor is usually working to focus the client solely on the addiction while the mental health provider is more likely to focus on the impact of trauma and its cognitive and emotional sequelae. When the target population is also poor or non-white—and predominantly female—the helping system's confusion increases and the recidivism of symptoms and behaviors escalates.

Many women with co-occurring trauma and mental health symptoms suffer such crippling addictions as alcohol and drug abuse, self-injury, eating disorders, and process addictions (self-sabotaging relationships, gambling, and other risk-taking compulsions). They are also tormented by the complex interactions between their trauma-based addiction and mental health conditions such as depression, anxiety, and personality disorders.

Services for Battered and/or Sexually Assaulted Women with Co-occurring Disorders

It is a major challenge to coordinate the treatment needs of anyone suffering the co-occurring disorder of trauma-based mental health and addiction symptoms. If we add in the experience of someone who is in need of services because of current violence in her life, the treatment route gets even more complicated. First, she will be directed to a program that deals with keeping her safe. She may need shelter or help with alternative housing; if she is a parent, she may need help with child care. Secondarily, if she is struggling with an addiction, she will be referred to addiction-focused services such as detoxification and residential treatment programs, and 12-step programs.

However, if she openly discloses her addiction she may be refused services in domestic violence (or homeless) facilities because her addiction could render others in the program unsafe. Thus, she may find that until she gives up her addiction, she cannot receive help for either her childhood trauma issues or her current violent living situation. Yet she is experiencing the continuous restimulation of her need to self-medicate because the triggers of her current violent situation amplify the mental health issues rooted in her childhood trauma experiences. Her life is a catch-22: She can't receive services as a battered woman until she abstains from her addiction. But because of the link between the current violence and the old ghosts of childhood violence, she can't give up her attempts at self-medication via her addiction.

These are predictable barriers to successful treatment and recovery for women with trauma-related mental health and addiction issues, compounded by current interpersonal violence or limited economic resources (both unfortunately frequent conditions for these women).

In addition, there is a set of treatment barriers pertaining to *lack of information*. There is a lack of education in each service sector regarding interactional components of trauma (both childhood and current domestic violence), addiction, and mental health issues. Professional service providers often lack information regarding peer support services (i.e., 12-step programs, domestic violence shelters and programs, women's centers), and peer support services conversely lack information about what professional providers can offer in group or individual psychotherapy.

There are barriers pertaining to *attitudes* and *territoriality*. Issues of attitude can include lack of support from State and Federal services for women who are on welfare because of the stigma of trauma, addiction, and mental health problems. Or there may be "turf" issues: Providers are often unused to collaborating with respect to co-occurring disorders. And there are often bureaucratic restrictions on services: diagnosis constraints, insurance coverage, etc.

There are also specific barriers associated with both *urban and rural poverty*. These include transportation, child care, lack of anonymity contributing to shame and secrecy, and limited amounts of beds and shelters for women and children.

The Need for a New Approach

Clearly, we need a model to bridge the gap between the domains of trauma-related addiction and mental health treatment. We need a model to provide a recovery program for women and girls with the mental health challenges presented by homelessness, domestic assault, and violence. The absence of clearly organized treatment protocols for this population has led to increasing numbers of women and their children cycling in and out of treatment programs and shelters. This creates financial burdens for Federal, State, and local governments, and enormous shame, pain, and hopelessness for the woman caught in this deadly struggle with her internal ghosts and a hostile environment. By offering a treatment protocol that creates a bridge to more effective engagement with existing addiction and mental health services, the ATRIUM model offers hope both to consumers and service providers.

It is the goal of this book to help create both a theoretical and a practical bridge between the worlds of addiction and mental health treatment, between the worlds of consumers and providers. Addiction specialists and mental health providers treating traumatized people need practical ways to communicate and collaborate across the paradigm gap. The ATRIUM approach provides useful ways to think about the co-occurring challenges of trauma and addiction, and practical assessment and intervention instructions to guide your work as a mental health provider, an addictions specialist, an advocate, a healthcare worker, and/or a survivor.

■Development and Theory of the ATRIUM Protocol

In response to the demand for an effective, integrated, and more holistically respectful response to the needs of trauma survivors, Dusty Miller's (1994; 1996) model of treatment for survivors of childhood abuse (the "Trauma Reenactment" model) was expanded and redesigned with the central aim of addressing the effects of trauma on both the mind and the body. Miller's original treatment model was redeveloped to include attention to the physical and spiritual as well as the psychological legacy of trauma.

A Bridge from the Past to the Present

The often devastating impact of childhood abuse demands a treatment response that addresses healing along the multiple dimensions impacted. ATRIUM serves as a powerful and temporally responsive synthesis of past and future thinking regarding effective trauma treatment. The ATRIUM protocol seeks to build a bridge between past history (the "trauma story") and current functioning within a context that progressively acknowledges, validates, and then effectively reconstructs the multiple pathways of Trauma Reenactment. Furthermore, by actively identifying and exploring the mind/body interface in relation to trauma, a more holistic understanding of trauma, as well as a more holistic treatment paradigm, is cultivated. As such, Miller's expanded TR model provides an effective biopsychosocial frame that is reflective of and can be responsive to the interrelated and often complex treatment needs of survivors of childhood trauma who struggle with addictions and mental health challenges.

Trauma Reenactment

Trauma Reenactment or TR (Miller, 1996; Miller, Guidry, & Daly, 1999; Miller et al., in press) is one of the problems that trauma creates. Trauma Reenactment explains a variety of self-harming behaviors. Many women, men, and adolescents find that learning to cope with the impact of trauma presents major mental health and addiction challenges; survivors of sexual and physical abuse are frequently in deep spiritual pain. The concept of Trauma Reenactment includes all of these physical, mental, and spiritual problems of daily living.

Sadly, many mental health professionals, addiction counselors, and peer advocates do not seem to grasp the scope of Trauma Reenactment. Women and children who are victims of interpersonal violence should be seen as brave casualties of a war or innocent bystanders caught up in a deadly epidemic illness, although most of the time they are not (Miller, 1994). Teenagers and adults are often blamed for their own despair, even their own death, because wounds are often inflicted by their own hands or their partners ("She's killing herself . . . Why doesn't she just eat?" or "She should have known better . . . Why didn't she leave him?" or "It's all in her head . . . She's just making herself sick"). These wounds are a consequence of earlier injuries inflicted by parents or other caretakers—wounds that never heal and can prove devastating for many or, for some, even deadly.

Thousands of girls and women suffer because they are caught in the cycle of Trauma Reenactment. Prisoners of TR, they tell painful stories of childhood physical and sexual abuse through their drug and alcohol addiction, anorexia, bulimia, self-injuries, somatic complaints, body-based illnesses, and abusive relationships.

Trauma Reenactment as Narrative

Trauma Reenactment can be understood as telling the story of harms done in childhood (Miller, 1994). It reinforces the deeply rooted belief that the woman is incapable of protecting herself because she was not protected in childhood. For many survivors of childhood trauma, it feels impossible to stop self-harming patterns like drug abuse or self-mutilation as they recreate the destruction of their abuser. Survivors may inexplicably fail to interrupt the cycle of returning to a violent partner as they reexperience the process of victimization. Trauma survivors who experience painful somatic distress of ambiguous origins and who continuously seek medical interventions often reenact their search for protection and healing that eluded them in childhood. Their pain, like their early experience of trauma, is real and not imaginary; it gives credence to their search for protection, which may originate from earlier unmet needs.

Whatever pattern of distress prevails, when someone cannot "just say no," and the cycle of self-harm, self-destruction, and self-sabotage repeats despite help from 12-step programs, battered women's organizations, medication, surgery, or talking to a counselor about childhood trauma, then he or she is probably engaged in a debilitating struggle with Trauma Reenactment (Miller, 1996).

Blaming the Victim

Trauma Reenactment is a baffling adversary because so many of its victims—mostly women and girls—seem to *choose* self-harmful lifestyles and behaviors. Many people close to these women, from doctors and counselors to family and friends, become angry or exasperated.

> Lynn's husband doesn't understand why she can't just go to AA and get sober like his brother and father did.

> Carol is transferred from doctors to therapists to hospital staff. "She has talked and talked about her childhood traumas—for years! She's hopeless as far as I'm concerned," says the doctor who admitted Carol for the third time to his ER unit after she seriously injured herself cutting and burning her skin.

> Jennifer relentlessly seeks treatment from her primary care physician for her mysterious, painful symptoms of fatigue and excruciating aching in her joints. She, too, has exasperated her doctor and others because of her seemingly untreatable medical condition.

These women all suffer from undiagnosed, unrecognized Trauma Reenactment and are further victimized by a helping system too often unable to address the roots of their pain.

Secret Behaviors of Trauma Reenactment

TR involves excessive secrecy: just as the abused child lived with dangerous secrets, so does the girl or woman who struggles with TR. She holds fast to secrets; she may even keep some from herself. Although it seems like a paradox, these behavioral manifestations often make sense to the person because it gives her the feeling of being the one who's in control of her own body. Strange as it may seem, patterns of TR behavior (alcoholic drinking, drugging, bingeing and purging, being in abusive relationships, chronic pain, and illness) often become the woman's "best friend" because Trauma Reenactment fools her into thinking that these ways of being are her best defense—it's her best chance at survival.

The types of trauma-related addictions and mental health issues considered to constitute Trauma Reenactment and included in the ATRIUM approach are:

- drug and alcohol abuse

- food addictions
- self-injury
- self-sabotaging relationships
- self-sabotaging behaviors like compulsive gambling, criminal behavior, and dangerous risk-taking behavior

A person who reenacts trauma may be addicted to a cluster of self-harmful behaviors. Using the ATRIUM approach, we understand these addictions as having been *the best ways the trauma survivor knows to express the painful dynamics of her trauma experience.* It is also how a survivor may choose to demonstrate that she is the one in control. At the same time, the ATRIUM model helps the survivor let go of these addictive behaviors and helps her find better ways to connect with her community and experience empowerment.

Understanding the logical and functional reasons for these manifestations of TR behavior allows the women (and those who care about them) to approach the problem of TR from a position of respect. Many girls and women feel that their connection to bulimia, addiction, or an abusive partner, is more "safe" than helping, protective relationships. For others, the somatic expression of their pain in the form of a medical condition can become a paradoxically comforting companion as well as the means to legitimize their search for protection and healing. To reiterate, the ATRIUM approach suggests that we understand TR as the best way a woman has found to continue to be in charge of her own body. "I choose to use drugs—no one's taking my choice away from me again," says one 16-year-old. It is also the best way the woman has found, so far, to tell the story of her pain.

The key to recognizing Trauma Reenactment is to understand the connection between the TR behavior and the person's unique story of childhood trauma. Some women and girls do things to their body that seem to literally represent what was done to them in childhood.

> **Sylvia** cuts and burns herself when relationships end. She has an extensive trauma history, including sadistic physical and sexual abuse. She was abandoned for long periods of time by her caretakers.

> **Crystal** hesitantly identifies herself as a trauma survivor but says, "It was really no big thing, some inappropriate stuff between my older brother and me, some creepy touching by my step dad." She is bulimic. Her choice of bulimia as Trauma Reenactment may be understood as Crystal's way of reenacting sickening intrusions that must be rejected (literally regurgitated).

> In a different presentation of Trauma Reenactment, **Judy** keeps returning to a relationship with a batterer. Her mother was an active alcoholic and she was beaten throughout her childhood.

Other women may not reenact their childhood trauma quite so literally. But they still tell the story of the relationships they experienced and how they learned to be with themselves.

Karla abuses both alcohol and prescription drugs to reenact the trauma of being verbally abused and emotionally abandoned by her parents. Trauma Reenactment traps her in an endless repetition of that story: Her drinking and drugging patterns reenact being victimized by neglect or nonprotective relationships.

Jan experiences chronic headaches and abdominal pain that is considered to have no clear organic basis by medical providers who have examined her. She, like other women imprisoned by TR, is often mistreated and invalidated by professionals who think she should be able to overcome her pain. Reflective of her early experience of abuse, her pain is minimized and her needs devalued. Once again she finds no protection, no safety, and no healing from those who are supposed to care for her.

■A New Treatment Model

Here are some important questions asked about the treatment of co-occurring trauma-related mental health and addiction challenges:

- Why do we need another trauma model?
- How can we address the problem of trauma when someone is actively addicted to substances, food, or any other self-harmful behavior? Won't talking about trauma just make the addiction worse?
- Can we use one integrated model for people who struggle with the effects of both trauma and addiction?

We believe that while there are many good trauma recovery models, there is a need for a model that concurrently addresses the problems of trauma-related addictions and mental health challenges. We also believe that using this integrated approach to trauma addiction is effective and that addressing the person's trauma issues does not automatically make the addiction worse. We believe that using ATRIUM will work well at the following junctures in a person's recovery process.

- It can be used in conjunction with other trauma recovery models, especially when addictions and self-harming behavior are involved.
- It can be used in partnership with other addiction models, often helping someone to more successfully engage in a 12-step program or other intervention aimed primarily at achieving abstinence.

- It can be used exclusively when someone is fearful, mistrustful, or otherwise unable to engage in addiction recovery programs—the goal would be to help someone become more comfortable about subsequently engaging in addiction recovery after graduating from the 12-week ATRIUM protocol.
- It can be used by a therapist or counselor as a structured, manualized format for advancing a client's individual work when the more traditional psychotherapy path seems to be at a standstill.

Does Trauma Reenactment Require Professional Intervention?

While there are many professionals who are able to help solve problems related to both trauma and addiction, this model—and the manual itself—have been developed from the assumptions that:

- survivors are experts concerning their own problems;
- survivors are very capable of establishing communities of care and are competent healers for themselves and their peer community; and
- Trauma Reenactment is a description, not a diagnosis—like all other peer-based healing models, this is a nonpathologizing model.

In this expanded version of the Trauma Reenactment model, some primary premises of the ATRIUM model are that: survivors not only reenact their early abuse by engaging in addictive, self-harming behavior or by recreating abusive and toxic relationships, but the legacy of early abuse can also emerge and be recreated in the life of a survivor within the *biological* (i.e., body-based or somatic) and *spiritual* domains as well.

Healing the Mind, Body, and Spirit

At present, treatment for childhood trauma emphasizes the cognitive and relational reworking of trauma-based beliefs and behaviors. Some of the most promising research in the development of trauma treatment, however, can be found in the resurgent interest in treating the impact of trauma on the survivor's somatic functioning. Bessel van der Kolk and other researchers (1996) have led the way in validating what trauma survivors themselves have told us for a long time: Trauma effects *both* the mind and the body in significant ways. Now both consumers and professionals are articulating the impact of earlier trauma on the survivor's overall physiological as well as cognitive and emotional functioning.

Trauma experts are also beginning to look at the effects of trauma on the survivor's social and spiritual life as well. A number of trauma experts (Barrett, 1999;

Herman, 1992b) talk about how important it is to consider ways to repair disrupted connections to community and shattered trust in spiritual dimensions of the survivor's life.

We need to understand how trauma impacts the mind, the body, and the spirit if we are going to be able to intervene in the powerful patterns of addiction recreated in Trauma Reenactment.

■Trauma and the Body

The effect of trauma on the central nervous system and the neurohormonal system is currently considered as important as impaired cognitive functioning and disturbed object relations; in fact, all are now seen as salient, interrelated factors in understanding and treating the sequelae of trauma. Contemporary research indicates that perhaps as many as 90 percent of those suffering with Somatization Disorders have histories of early trauma. This means that 90 percent of people who have chronic physical pain or illness that can't be explained in simple medical terms may have suffered trauma in their past. Many trauma survivors also recreate harmful effects to their bodies through drug and alcohol abuse, in eating disorders, and through self-injury.

Trauma Reenactment Expanded: The Biological Foundation

Whether it is in the form of self-harmful behaviors, physically abusive relationships, or chronic somatization, Trauma Reenactment can often be characterized by repetitive distress at the physiological level. In working with Trauma Reenactment, we have found it essential to educate both survivors and professionals about the ways in which trauma permanently alters physiological functioning and thus gets "stuck" in the adult's behavioral and emotional functioning. We offer the following brief and basic review of how an original traumatic experience may impact the body.

The Fight or Flight Response

Canon (1932) first identified the generalized response to situations perceived as threatening that has come to be known as the "fight or flight" response. This universal response to fearful stimuli is seen as functionally adaptive and is found to be mediated through the sympathetic branch of the autonomic nervous system. The fight or flight response is a full-body, systemwide response with multiple physiological expressions that include, but are not limited to, an increase in heart rate, blood pressure, muscular tension, sweat gland activity, dilation of the pupils, constriction of the peripheral vascular system, and increased levels of norepinephrene and epinephrene (also known as noradrenalin and adrenaline). We now know that this response occurs in order for us to respond more effectively in situations that present as significant threats.

The fight or flight response represents a traditional model of stress that emphasizes the short-term, adaptive response to an acute, adverse stressor. In reaction to a stressful event, internal resources that promote self-preservation are activated. Following a stressful event, the individual returns to a homeostatic state. The heightened physiological response pattern present during the stressful event diminishes and ultimately abates. A person's physiological functioning returns to baseline as the heightened bodily response is no longer needed for the individual's survival. In this model, failure to return a prior level of functioning following a stressful event is seen as a failure to adapt effectively.

Traumatic Stress Response

What happens when the stressful event exceeds an individual's capacity to adapt effectively? The traumatic stress response is the current model used to aid in understanding the effects of overwhelming traumatic experiences upon individuals (van der Kolk, McFarlane, & Weisaeth, 1996). The traumatic stress response can be understood as that response to an aversive stimulus or experience (either acute or long-term) that so overwhelms an individual that the normative fight or flight response becomes dysregulated and the individual's capacity to return to homeostasis becomes impaired. Adaptation is not at issue under these conditions because the adaptive mechanism itself can be seen as having sustained damage that circumvents effective functioning.

Let us briefly examine two clinical phenomena, dissociation and intrusive memories (or flashbacks), associated with both the adaptive fight or flight response as well as the development of pathology following traumatic experiences. Many of us who have had close brushes with death or witnessed the near or tragic loss of another may recall the surreal experience of watching oneself from a distance or the unusual absence of any emotion at the height of the traumatic event. Dissociation, or the splitting off of cognition, affect, and, in extreme cases, the separation of the self from integrated conscious awareness, occurs at the height of the fight or flight response. Much research indicates that there appears to be a significant positive relationship between increased levels of physiological arousal and increased levels of dissociation (van der Kolk et al., 1996). One hypothesis links this occurrence to the release of endogeneous opioids in order to mediate pain and fear during an event perceived as life-threatening

(Pittman, van der Kolk, Orr, & Greenberg, 1990). This dissociative response has proven to be adaptive in the moment of acute stress and usually abates when the threat has passed. However, in response to a stressor that exceeds the viability of one's systemic adaptability and precludes effective coping, an individual may develop a generalized hyperarousal response to stimuli reminiscent of the traumatic event. As a result, an individual can repeatedly experience inappropriate levels of hyperarousal to neutral stimuli that can subsequently trigger dissociative states. The repetitive, uncontrollable occurrence of dissociative states as a result of trauma has been known to contribute to the development of a range of dissociative disorders and comorbid conditions (van der Kolk et al., 1996).

Likewise, intrusive memories of a traumatic event are viewed as an adaptive attempt to synthesize and integrate an experience that was largely perceived in a heightened physiological, and therefore altered, state of consciousness. In most cases these unbidden memories diminish within 48–72 hours following the trauma and homeostasis is restored. However, for some individuals this unbidden and terrifying reexperiencing of the traumatic events continues unabated. As a result, a retraumatizing cycle is set into motion that involves the intense reexperiencing of the trauma through flashbacks. This experience of reliving the trauma leads to the triggering of the fight or flight response in reaction to the intrusive memory along with the activation of all the physiological sequelae that accompanied the original event. As noted earlier, heightened physiological arousal can lead to dissociative experiences, withdrawal, and the failure to integrate the event into conscious awareness. This agonizing cycle gets perpetuated in such a way that the once normative and adaptive fight or flight response becomes a maladaptive, dysregulated, and "hard-wired" reaction that is erroneously triggered, perpetuates systemic overload, and is extremely difficult to extinguish. This phenomenon is understood clinically in the expression of PTSD, of which intrusive symptoms represent a marked identifier.

Traumatic Stress and the Brain

Recent innovations in the study of the brain have yielded intriguing information regarding how the brain functions during times of stress. Briefly, what has been discovered is that the fight or flight response is said to be triggered by the amygdala in the brain before the information gets fully processed and organized. A short-cut between neurological systems occurs under situations of emotional stress and physiological hyperarousal so that the sensory and emotional aspects of an event can be stored in memory before they have a chance to be accurately categorized and fully integrated by the higher order brain functions. As such, the memory of a traumatic event processed at a time of heightened physiological arousal is thought to be processed differently than those memories, which occur under more normal, everyday circumstances. This finding has broad implications for understanding the diverse response to traumatic events that is evident among clinical populations. Of particular interest, however, is the idea that the traumatic memory, not fully integrated cognitively or affectively, often finds its expression in somatic complaints. The effects of overwhelming trauma are now being understood not only in terms of psychological fallout, but also in terms of the psycho-physical sequelae that mobilizes in the body and manifests somatically. The following provides a brief exploration of how trauma, presenting within the medical healthcare arena, can find expression in a variety of physical ailments.

Somatization and the Body

One of the most recent developments in the understanding of traumatic sequelae is a growing awareness of trauma reenactment through somatization. Research indicates that large numbers of trauma survivors present in medical settings. These patients often present as medical conundrums, displaying a wide range of intense somatic concerns with vague or ill-defined origins and variable manifestations. In a survey of over 500 women in a primary care health center, Lechner and colleagues (1993) found that 26 percent of female patients reported childhood sexual abuse. In addition, the variable most associated with a history of childhood abuse was the number of somatic complaints with survivors of abuse reporting 2–3 times the rate of medical complaints of women who were not abused. These medical problems covered multiple systems—respiration, gastrointestinal, neurological, gynecological, and musculoskeletal.

In specialty care settings such as gynecological practices or gastrointestinal clinics, these statistics double. Moeller, Bachman, and Moeller (1993) surveyed almost 700 women in a gynecological practice regarding demographic information, family history, physical and psychological health in addition to stressful events and abusive experiences in childhood. Over half (53 percent) reported one of three identified kinds of abuse: physical, sexual, or psychological. Eighteen percent reported two kinds and 5 percent reported all three types of abuse. The greater number of types of abuse, the more problems women reported. In research derived from female patients presenting gastrointestinal (GI) concerns, Drossmen and colleagues (1990) found that 44 percent of over 200 patients surveyed also reported having a history of sexual trauma, either in childhood or as an adult. Patients with "functional" (or medically unexplained) irritable bowel syndrome had even higher rates of reported abuse. More recently, Leserman and colleagues (1996) found that 66 percent of women with GI symptoms also had physical or sexual abuse histories.

The Body and Trauma-based Addictions

When survivors reenact their trauma experience through addictions to drugs, alcohol, and food, they are often frustrated by their failure to find relief through addiction programs that do not address the interaction between the body's memory of trauma and the effect of the addiction.

Although it was unquestionably beneficial for alcoholics and addicts to be seen as suffering from a disease rather than judged as deviant, criminal, or generically "bad," the disease model has perhaps placed too great an emphasis on the genetic etiology of addictions. Many trauma survivors found that in 12-step and other "disease model" programs, they were discouraged from talking about the origins of their addictions and told instead that it was simply a genetic inheritance. Talking about the connection between drinking or drugging and past abuse was generally forbidden in the 12-step meetings of the past, right through the '80s. Even in some 12-step meetings today it is not considered especially helpful for addicts and alcoholics in recovery to talk about their abusive childhoods. The disease model emphasizes "here and now" stories: The formula is to describe the past distressing history of substance abuse, the discovery of one's identity as an alcoholic or addict, and the positive changes derived from attending 12-step meetings—getting a sponsor, "working the steps," and accepting the help of one's "Higher Power."

While we wholeheartedly support the many positive healing aspects of 12-step programs, we believe that trauma survivors need support in connecting their addictions to their traumatic histories. Addictions are known to be more prevalent in some families than others, just as some cultural groups are more impacted by addictions than others, thus supporting the "disease theory." Yet it is also true that trauma survivors may use addictive behaviors as a direct result of their abuse. Both genetic predisposition and a history of interpersonal abuse may be important for the trauma survivor to understand.

What may be most important about the connection between addictive behaviors and a trauma history is the likelihood of relapse. Even when there is support to help trauma survivors give up their addictive behavior(s), relapse rates are high. We believe that high relapse rates may occur because the power of Trauma Reenactment is not fully understood by those who seek to help the survivor. Survivors may experience relapse because they have not been allowed to understand their addiction as a powerful way of coping with the legacy of their abuse.

In the ATRIUM approach, work is done to help each survivor understand *why she has had trouble in the past* giving up her addiction. ATRIUM offers new tools for understanding how the addictive behavior reenacts the earlier abuse. The model develops new ways to help people utilize community support in their efforts to move forward without reverting to their addictive behaviors.

Understanding Mind-Body Interactions

ATRIUM explains the ways in which the effects of trauma can emerge in the body as well as mental and social dimensions. How the survivor behaviorally reenacts her history, how the trauma impacts her physical functioning as well as her relationships and her cognitive schema, are all important recovery concerns.

ATRIUM fosters effective coping skills and provides an innovative approach to treatment for the dysregulated mind-body interactions. In the past, survivors have been forced to doubt their own reality in regard to what they experience in their bodies. Many survivors, through shame and self-doubt, have suffered their body-based experiences in profound isolation. The psychoeducational component of this recovery model counteracts this by concretely validating and universalizing these experiences.

> Jill was moved to tears following an explanation of the traumatic stress response and a review of some of the research regarding the biological impact of trauma. With tears streaming down her face she said, "You mean there really is something wrong physically? I'm not making up this stuff that's been happening in my body for the past 30 years?" Jill experienced significant relief when her personal experience was reflected in the current understanding of how trauma impacts the mind/body. She also felt less alone because others in the group shared similar self-doubts in relation to their body experiences. And she was able to learn new skills that allowed her to experience control of her body for the first time in her life.

Process components of the ATRIUM model offer multilayered opportunities for reflection on the way group members experience their trauma-related symptoms. In conjunction with this reflective process, opportunities are offered to reconsider and reframe current experience.

For example, during a group discussion related to physical pain and illness, group members shared their understanding of the dominant paradigm in Western culture regarding pain: common idioms such as "No pain, no gain," "It can't be that bad," and "It's all in your head" are among the central messages survivors often receive when they attempt to describe their physical symptoms. Once these blaming and shaming messages are examined, the group participants can explore what kinds of responses they would have found more helpful.

■Trauma and the Mind

In mental health system settings, the impact of trauma on the mind has been identified with problems like dissociation, flashbacks, and cognitive confusion (racing or jumbled thoughts). Trauma has also been understood to affect the mind through emotional problems like depression, anxiety, rage, and feelings of chronic emptiness. In the ATRIUM approach, the interaction between mind and body is explored on two levels. The mind and the body are connected through a focus on traumatic stress (see session 1). Cognitive (mental health) problems like depression, anxiety, and rage are viewed through a lens connecting these current states of mind with relational problems created by childhood trauma.

> Mary says that when she experiences high levels of anxiety, the ATRIUM protocol helps her understand that her basic biological "wiring" has been affected by her early experiences of traumatic stress. The model also helps her to learn new ways of coping with the uncomfortable symptoms of anxiety through mindfulness meditation, deep breathing, and engagement in different forms of exercise.

> When Julie is labeled as suffering from depression, the ATRIUM model also helps her make the connection between her experience of earlier trauma and her fear of trusting or getting close to others. She learns that her body reacts to her trauma history through a numbing or feeling of sluggishness, her mind responds with sadness and self-doubt, and her spirit responds with despair and isolation.

Viewing a woman's experience this way, an emotional problem like depression is viewed as "3-D distress," a concept that encompasses the impact of trauma on the mind, body, and spirit.

Connecting trauma and problems previously labeled as "mental" or "emotional" with patterns of addiction is also an important part of the ATRIUM approach. Many people who use substances addictively are given mental health labels like "thought-disordered" or "psychotic." Sometimes substance abuse creates this psychotic presentation of the "disordered" thoughts; sometimes a legacy of trauma or current traumatic violence can produce the same effect. ATRIUM helps both survivors and professionals to understand that these co-occurring challenges work together to create a very confusing picture of what someone is actually capable of achieving.

> Amber had been given a mental health diagnosis of "Depression, with psychotic features," by a therapist who had been assigned to her after her second hospitalization; earlier, she had been diagnosed as having Schizophrenia. She was taught by the mental health system that she would never be able to participate as a competent adult in the world and that she would also be unable to have mature intimate relationships. Through participating in the ATRIUM protocol, Amber was able to stop using addictive drugs and alcohol, and after doing some in-depth work in individual psychotherapy with a sensitive trauma-informed therapist, she is fully engaged in a peer advocate job and is continuing a satisfying relationship.

■ Trauma and the Spirit

Although most people who have experienced childhood abuse and most who have studied it can agree that trauma creates major challenges in terms of the survivor's spiritual well-being, few models specifically address the centrality of spirituality in recovery. The 12-step program approach offers a notable exception: The connection to one's Higher Power is emphasized, playing what we believe to be one of the most successful parts in helping people achieve recovery from their addictions. Most mental health professionals, however, are trained to separate spiritual healing from mental and physical health practices. It is notable that in many indigenous cultures, healing from emotional or mental problems involves primary input from spiritual healers, just as many of these cultures have never separated healing the mind from healing the body!

Mary Jo Barrett, a family therapist who has worked for many years with large numbers of clients with trauma histories, has emphasized the centrality of healing the spirit. In her groundbreaking article on healing from trauma (1999), she states: "Trauma interrupts emotional, psychological, *spiritual*, sexual, and/or intellectual development and chronically or acutely impinges on a person's ability to cope or function" (p. 193). She goes on to describe profound changes in her clients: "It became clear that the process of change had tapped a divine spark in the majority of the clients we interviewed. This does not necessitate a belief in God. It necessitates a desire to feel and be something and someone different. Treatment had enabled the clients to envision the world and themselves differently" (p. 195).

Research by Janice Dreshman-Chiodo (1997) examined the effects of participation in "spiritual" groups in relation to the healing process for individual clients. The study found statistical significance between well-being and childhood trauma, suggesting that individuals with a higher sense of well-being may have been better able to withstand the trauma and that participation in the groups led to increased feelings of belonging, a sense of community, a sense of unity with the environment, and increased connectedness with others.

The ATRIUM approach considers healing the spirit equally as important as healing the body and mind. Spiritual distress is viewed as a breakdown in connection with the larger community, as well as a feeling of pervasive despair, an unwillingness to trust, and a breakdown of faith. "Spirit" may mean fellowship, love, and friendship or a relationship with God, Goddess, Higher Power, or perhaps Nature. However it is described, it is understood as a process through which complete healing means renewed hope through a reconnection with a meaningful community. The model encourages survivors to make healing connections with each other and with nonhuman sources of support (pets, plants, Nature). Through these potentially less threatening nonpower-based relationships, a renewed faith in a loving community may repair shattered trust and faith.

In the ATRIUM approach consistent connections are made in every group session to relationship and spiritual challenges. No matter what the topic of concern may be, it is always viewed as it relates to distress in relationships and hopelessness in spiritual connectedness. Group members are invited to discuss their past spiritual struggles and are given new skills as well as new experiences to enable them to know the joy of successful relationships and spiritual healing.

Addressing the Trauma History

Recovering and re-storying traumatic memories are hallmarks of most trauma recovery models. The ATRIUM protocol also works with trauma memories, but the sequence and emphasis differs from many other models. Rather than working toward the goal of uncovering or retrieving trauma memories, we believe that the focus needs to be on how these memories have impacted the survivor's mind, body, and spirit. Survivors suffering from addictions and body-based distress stemming from their traumas hold their trauma memories in their bodies, in their current relationships, and in spiritual hopelessness. Rather than functioning like detectives to glean the "facts" of childhood abuse, survivors and their allies work together to understand the connections between trauma memories and the ways the trauma stories are retold through the use of substances, disordered eating, self-injury, somatic complaints, and hurtful relationships.

The re-storying of the survivor's childhood in the ATRIUM model emphasizes strengths, coping capacities, and resilience that can be remembered or rediscovered throughout the individual's history. ATRIUM values the retelling of positive relationships and personal strengths rather than dwelling on the pain and horror of the traumatic experiences. We have found that most survivors are triggered by their own and other survivor's horror stories, which can amplify all the addictive behaviors the survivor uses to cope with being flooded and disheartened. Instead of reliving these nightmarish memories, survivors are reassured that they have not imagined their abuse but that it is more useful to focus on understanding the impact of the memories and then to learn new ways to cope and to connect with other survivors.

The Triadic Self and the Protective Presence

Although the ATRIUM model offers a different way of approaching the memories of childhood abuse, there is room for survivors to review the painful legacy of being abused through a unique concept called the **Triadic Self** (Miller, 1994), which is a way of telling the story of being abused and not being protected. It is central to the model, and is revisited throughout the 12-week protocol, deepening the understanding of how trauma and addictions are enacted and then transformed through exercises designed to help change the woman's relationship with mind, body, and spirit.

Protection as the Central Trauma Reenactment Issue

Not being protected often seems to hurt even more than getting abused. The cycle of Trauma Reenactment is a story about the **Victim**, the **Abuser**, and the **Nonprotecting Bystander**, the usual actors in the childhood trauma scenario. This scenario is enacted in a variety of ways, including a woman's abusive relationship with a partner, her repetitive chronic pain, or her more active self-harming behaviors.

> Ruth may be enacting these dynamics when she binges and purges. She may have an internal struggle with herself when she becomes obsessed with her boyfriend. Fearing dependency and acute vulnerability, Ruth switches instead to becoming obsessed with her craving to binge. As she begins the binge part of the cycle, she is simultaneously saying "I have to have this whole cake" (the voice of the Abuser) and "No, I don't want to do this to myself" (the voice of the Victim). When she says to herself, "But I can't help it, I have to do it, I just can't stop myself," she is also playing the role of the Nonprotecting Bystander (the person[s] who didn't protect her in childhood).

In working to interrupt the deadly impact of the Triadic Self's Trauma Reenactment, it is essential to understand that the Triadic Self is using the woman's body to tell the story of earlier trauma. The woman needs to first understand that she, not the Triadic Self, is in control of her body. Eventually she will be able to work with her helping community to develop an internalized sense of what Miller (1994) has named the **Protective Presence**, thereby replacing the power of the destructive Triadic Self. The development and emergence of the Protective Presence is one of the most central tasks addressed in the Trauma Reenactment treatment model. Somewhat akin to the Higher Power of 12-step programs, the Protective Presence can be whatever amalgam of protective relationships the individual chooses for herself. When the work of the ATRIUM model is completed, the survivor is able to call upon a strong internal experience of her own unique Protective Presence and also to operationalize this in her work to support other survivors in their recovery.

■Structure of the Treatment Model

The ATRIUM protocol is organized in four sections that guide you through the three stages of Miller's original Trauma Reenactment model. These sections are designed to be used in a 12-week sequence, either in a group or individual-oriented format. A woman who does not have a group or a helper to do the work with her could use the manual by herself by following the suggested order. The four sections are as follows:

1. Three sessions to orient the user to the theory of Trauma Reenactment; the role of traumatic stress in connecting the problems of trauma, addiction, and mental health; and an introduction to the construct of the Triadic Self and the Protective Presence.

2. Three sessions that address the impact of Trauma Reenactment on the mind. This section covers the major mental health conditions of depression and grief, anger, fear, and anxiety. Addictions are addressed as they are often present in these emotional states.

3. Three sessions that address the impact of Trauma Reenactment on the body and how Trauma Reenactment is expressed in the body through somatic distress (illness and chronic pain), how the legacy of trauma affects the ways women view their bodies (body image), and how trauma is reenacted through the ways women experience touch and physical intimacy.

4. The last three sessions focus on Trauma Reenactment and the spirit, especially as spiritual well-being is understood as being in community. All three sessions address relationships—with children, partners, friends, helpers, and with nature and animals.

The unfolding of the trauma material occurs at each stage of the treatment model. Moving more or less sequentially through three major stages of treatment, the model provides a multilevel approach. Behaviors, cognitions, and relational capacities are equally important. This is a strength-based model, focusing on the survivor's assets versus her deficits. ATRIUM emphasizes the survivor as the primary expert concerning her problems and her capacity to change. The model respects the many levels at which the survivor's symptoms and relational issues tell the story of her traumatic experiences. The goal for treatment is to help survivors find less painful ways to express their life stories so that they may leave Trauma Reenactment behind.

The Outer Circle

In the first stage, or "Outer Circle," information is gathered about the context of each survivor's life as influenced by both trauma and experiences of help-seeking. Family rules, myths, beliefs, and stories, especially pertaining to the history of problems, helping experiences, and solutions provide information necessary to construct a more useful narrative about each individual in her past and current relational contexts. It is important to remember that the stories about helping relationships may be about both negative and positive experiences. *The survivor may have as many stories about helping others as she does about receiving help.*

The survivors' stories are supplemented with psychoeducational information about trauma's effect on the biological (neurohormonal) systems as well as the impact of trauma in dictating many of the emotional and spiritual events in their daily lives. It is also in the Outer Circle that spiritual disconnections are first identified and connected to the survivors' trauma history. All of this psychoeducational work centers in teaching survivors about the construct of Trauma Reenactment and helping them to identify how they reenact trauma specifically in their own lives.

In this early stage of treatment, revisiting trauma memories is not the central ingredient of the recovery process. As much as possible, group leaders actively block the disclosure of abuse memories and try to limit disclosures of traumatic current events or symptoms. As has already been explained, our belief is that disclosing and listening to the disclosures of other survivors may be upsetting for the survivor when she has not yet begun to learn new ways to cope with distress. Group participants have not yet established a deep enough relationship with the group (or in the case of an individual using the manual while working with an individual helper, the survivor has not yet really connected deeply with her counselor or advocate) to risk being vulnerable in this way. There is not yet a clear enough treatment history, especially in terms of the survivor's previous failed attempts to feel understood, accepted, and protected in relation to abuse issues. In addition, the survivor has not had enough time to observe and assess the helping persons' relational capabilities—those capacities which would make telling the trauma narrative safe for her.

The most important reason to block the rehashing of early traumatic material in the initial stages of treatment is based on our understanding of how the biological impact of early trauma is restimulated by recalling trauma memories. Rather than stir up the physiological distress recreated by the retelling of distressing memories, the focus is instead on the ways the survivors have been doing their best *currently* to deal with the legacy of trauma.

It is important to learn about each survivor's resilience as well as her struggles with the painful legacy of trauma. In the Outer Circle, it is useful to find out how other helping professionals, family members, and community have been beneficial (or not) so that we know what works well and what doesn't work for each individual.

The Middle Circle

During the second, or "Middle Circle," stage of treatment, problems and symptoms are addressed more directly. Storytelling is done in a larger contextual system in which the physical, emotional, and spiritual reenactments of trauma continue to be addressed from a psychological and spiritual level. Survivors begin a more concentrated effort to connect more effectively with peer support resources, such as relevant 12-step recovery groups and—if necessary—professional systems (i.e., medical health care professionals, treatment hospitals, legal systems, school personnel).

While the emphasis in the Middle Circle is the successful building of a support system, a variety of specific trauma-based problems are addressed. Survivors deepen their understanding of how trauma has impacted them at the 3-D (mind-body-spirit) level. They are given new information and new coping skills to help them change their patterns of addiction, self-harm, and distress in relationships.

The most important task of Middle Circle work is to create a support system so that when the women choose to explore or rework their trauma stories, they do not face the reminders of painful, shameful experiences alone. As they connect their addictions and other distressing symptoms, thoughts, or behaviors to past abuse, they continue to build a support network that will sustain them through the work of the Inner Circle and beyond.

The Middle Circle task of creating connections to sustain the survivor is enriched by the psychoeducational work and the process work. Learning new information and practicing new coping skills continues as the ATRIUM protocol moves through the sessions about Trauma Reenactment and the mind and body. Survivors learn that they are not alone in their shame and pain. They work continually on new coping skills to enable them to be more present. They are getting ready to do the work in the last stage of the protocol, which is the deepening of relationships and the connection to community through a focus on healing the spirit.

The Inner Circle

In the final stage of the model, we move to the Inner Circle. Although the building of community is central, an important part of the Inner Circle is to deepen the internalized representations of the childhood trauma-based relationships—the concept of the Triadic Self. As connections with other survivors, helpers, and spiritual healing takes hold, the central task of externalizing and replacing the Nonprotecting Bystander can really begin to feel possible. *Whether the survivor is a child or an adult, the heart of trauma is in the crying out for a protecting, loving parent and finding that no one responds.* Survivors are encouraged to share the awareness that they never really feel safe or experience a full connection to another without protecting relationships to incorporate as part of the self.

Survivors understand that they all share the experience of suffering an unrequited longing for protection. This may lead the survivor to enact the protecting role compulsively, excessively, hoping somehow to take it inside by either *giving* it again and again to others or *seeking* it again and again from others.

The Inner Circle involves guiding women to identify more clearly the internalized Abuser, the Nonprotecting Bystander, and the Victim in relation to current self-sabotaging patterns as well as in the context of historical dynamics being reenacted. Having learned to separate and externalize these "selves," the survivor is then able to gradually develop her own Protective Presence in place of the Nonprotecting Bystander. This first happens by the repetitive experience of thinking of the group, supportive friends, or any helping relationships as dependable representations of the Protective Presence. Survivors learn how to internalize these relationships, especially those formed within the group, and trust that eventually they will develop a solid sense of their own capacities to self-protect. The development of the internal Protective Presence eventually allows the survivor to feel in control of the internalized Abuser so she can relinquish TR manifestations such as addictive behaviors, abusive relationships, and even somatic illness.

A Guide to the 12-Week ATRIUM Protocol

The ATRIUM protocol helps trauma survivors with addictions and other self-harmful patterns learn why they have difficulty overcoming these behaviors and moving into deeper, more satisfying relationships with others, themselves, and their universe. It is also a helpful introduction to other modes of healing and recovery, from success in 12-step programs to community activism to trauma-informed psychotherapy. It can be used in conjunction with other interventions, including pharmaceutical drugs, longer term trauma-focused treatment, and occasionally day treatment or inpatient hospitalization when necessary. It is a model that can be utilized by trained professionals and paraprofessionals, and it can be adapted from this manual for use by individuals who do not have access to an ATRIUM group or any other group support options. However, we believe that people with TR issues would benefit greatly from group support.

Whether you are in the helper role, or looking for guidance in your own healing process, this model is designed to be "multilingual" (using both mental health and addiction parlance). The manual is written for both the professional and the consumer, accessible to those beginning the healing or recovery path and, we believe, equally useful for those who already have begun the work of abstinence from addictions and are reworking trauma-based mental health issues.

Each session of the 12-week model appears as a separate chapter of the manual. In keeping with the three stages of the model (which correspond with mind, body and spirit components), the first three sessions are considered the Outer Circle phase of the work. In this module information about traumatic stress and Trauma Reenactment is first introduced. The group shares their previous experience of seeking help—both successes and failures—and their history of helping others. It is also in this module that group members begin to get more connected to each other and to the group leaders, providing an opportunity to initially review relationship issues and begin to address hopelessness and shattered trust in spiritual resources.

Sessions 4–12 cover the work of the Middle and Inner Circles. These sessions focus on directly addressing problematic behaviors, building better support systems, focusing on improved relationships, and reworking the trauma memories so that the survivor can relinquish Trauma Reenactment and move forward with life.

The group ends with a celebration of each person's individual achievements and the strength of the group's increasing capacity to provide support to each other. The final "graduation" exercise involves passing on what each person wants to offer to other survivors who will join subsequent groups and begin the next "generation" of recovery.

Each ATRIUM group session has a topic that is central to the lives of most trauma survivors. At the end of the 12 weeks, the group may add a topic or two that is of special concern to them if it has not been addressed in the topics included in the manual.

Each session is organized in the following way:

1. Overview for Group Leaders (or individual counselors), which familiarizes them with the general issues covered in the session.
2. Group Leaders' Tasks: a checklist to help leaders see in a glance what they should be doing in that session.
3. Group Member Goals: another helpful checklist.
4. Guided Relaxation Exercise and Check-In.
5. Didactic Component—a brief text used to help survivors understand the relationship of their trauma to their problematic behaviors, addictions patterns, relational challenges, etc.
6. Process Component—guidelines to help group leaders with the usual process discussion that follows the didactic component.
7. Experiential Component—instructions for group leaders/counselors on how to work with an experiential exploration of the topic. For example, after teaching the group about traumatic stress and its impact on the body, the experiential segment teaches the group new ways to achieve relaxation through deep breathing.
8. Maintenance—group leaders help the group plan ways to practice new skills in the week that follows.

9. Helpful Hints, which help group leaders anticipate and troubleshoot potential areas of difficulty in the group process.
10. Handouts for group members encapsulating what they have covered in the session (all handouts are included separately and in order at the back of this manual).

Using a Didactic Approach

Trauma survivors often suffer from inadequate information about the effects of trauma on the body, mind, and spirit. In keeping with the trend of the twenty-first century to present specific information to mental health consumers, ATRIUM uses a didactic component in each session so that survivors can better understand why it is that they have felt out of control, alone, confused, disconnected from their bodies, hopeless, and frustrated in their relationships. On a more positive note, the group explores why survivors may have special abilities to know how others feel and think, why they are so sensitive to the suffering of others, and why they are especially well-suited to help others struggling with issues of trauma and addiction.

In the group model, part of every session is a learning component that allows survivors to feel less alone and more in charge of what is happening to them. They are being trained in this model to be better advocates for themselves and for others.

Using Expressive Therapy

The expressive component of each group session, which often involves drawing, writing, music, and movement (usually in some combination) weaves information, skills, personal process, and healing concepts together in a way that is personally meaningful and more deeply integrated by each group member.

The following exercise offers survivors a more experiential and personal level of exploring issues of self-image: Group members are invited to draw a representation of the pain carried in the body on one side of a blank "paper doll" figure. After sharing and discussion, members are then invited to draw or write images or words of healing and comfort in the same areas of the body on the reverse side of the paper doll. This powerful exercise enables each individual to express and acknowledge her pain in a validating environment. At the same time, she has the opportunity to begin the process of transforming not only her pain, but her relationship to pain, by utilizing a simple expressive format.

The Protective Presence is explored along several different dimensions in order to foster maximum therapeutic effect. The idea (or cognitive map) of the Protective Presence is presented in a psychoeducational format to the group while internalization of the Protective Presence is cultivated expressively. This session begins with a didactic discussion about how the Protective Presence can be developed to replace the self-harming cycles of the internalized Triadic Self. Group members then participate in an expressive exercise designed to facilitate the visualization and internalization of a source of comfort to be accessed in times of duress. Music is played as members develop their own personal gesture or movement to symbolize the source of comfort they are creating. The gentle movements or gestures become increasingly spontaneous as the exercise repeats. Repetition allows each individual to be the true source of creating and accessing comfort and safety. Repetition also serves to reinforce the integration of a central treatment concept in such a way as to foster its active use to self-soothe and prevent self-harm.

■Guidelines for ATRIUM Faciliators (Group Leaders and/or Therapists, Counselors, Advocates)

You will probably find that you need the same amount of time to plan each session as it takes to actually do the session, (i.e., 90 minutes of planning time and 90 minutes to do the work of each session with participants). Whether or not you can spend 90 minutes planning every week, group leaders need to plan time together to do the following.

- Familiarize yourselves with all the didactic components of each session.
- Practice the experiential components of each session by trying them out before asking the group to participate.
- Share with each other how each topic impacts you personally: *This is especially important for group leaders who are also survivors of abuse.*
- Briefly discuss how each group member is doing and plan for any special attention needed for a particular group member. However, group leaders are cautioned not to spend a lot of extra time with any individual group member either during or between group sessions, but to instead try to get group members to connect with each other: *The most important work of this model is to build strong communities of care locally rather than build dependence on group leaders.*
- Create a soothing, healing atmosphere in the meeting room: For example, a flower or plant in the center of the room will help with breathing and relaxation exercises; a well-functioning sound system will help with smooth flow in experiential components of each session, etc.

Why We Prefer Co-Led Groups

There are many reasons why ATRIUM is particularly well-suited to a group format and as many reasons why these groups should be co-led. Although many trauma survivors, like many women with addictions, feel intense shame and distrust, which leads them to say that they do not want to be part of a group to do their recovery work, we have learned from our own recovery experience that groups are the most important place to do this work. This is because each woman comes to realize that she is not alone and that other women suffer the same feelings of shame, anger, mistrust, and hopelessness. Yet these other women are finding their way, step by step, along the path to health and connection. When a woman who lives with Trauma Reenactment sees the woman sitting next to her has the same problems, she is offered the opportunity to diminish both her sense of shame and her degree of hopelessness and isolation. She is also offered the chance, over and over, to help someone else at the same time that she is learning how to help herself so she can feel—throughout the process of recovery—that she has something to *give* as well as receive the healing and acceptance she needs.

We believe that survivors are "local experts," and so it is important to have co-leaders who themselves are engaged in recovery from Trauma Reenactment. While some co-leaders are also trained professionals, we think it is very important whenever possible to have paraprofessionals co-lead groups with professionals to help the professionally trained facilitator be respectful and aware of each participant's struggle. Even if a professional facilitator has herself struggled with addictions and the legacy of trauma, her professional training can sometimes get in the way of her respect for the strength and resilience of the women she works with, and this is when the wisdom of the "local expert" may be especially helpful.

Ideally, leading an ATRIUM group provides an excellent resource to gain new helping skills and knowledge. We also know that many ATRIUM facilitators will bring the gift of personal experience with addictions and trauma-related mental health challenges. When one group leader is professionally trained and the other isn't, we caution the team to be mindful of hierarchical patterns of behavior. For example, the leaders may notice that they consistently privilege the professional's judgment about how to respond to an overactive group member when, in fact, the paraprofessional's ideas are just as useful. Also, when there are two leaders, they can trade off tasks. One can be the observer, responding to what group members are communicating (both verbally and nonverbally), while the other directs an exercise, leads a process discussion, or teaches the didactic material. And when a particular topic or someone's response in the group is upsetting or triggering for one facilitator, the other can play a more active role during the group as well as provide empathic support to her co-leader after a session.

The Intake Meeting

The process for enrolling people in ATRIUM focuses primarily on sharing information about the model rather than "screening" applicants (accepting or rejecting them for group membership). Intake sessions should take approximately an hour. We have found that it is more comfortable for women if the two group leaders meet with them in small groups of two or three rather than meeting with one woman at a time. This seems to work better both for the women and the group leaders: The women seem less nervous—less overpowered than if they were sitting alone with two facilitators being asked questions they may be feeling anxious about answering—and it also gives the women an opportunity to observe the facilitators more easily. In these small groups, the women can feel that they have choices about how to begin the process of allowing the facilitators to get to know them. The facilitators get the chance to meet all potential group members rather than dividing them up for individual intakes if time is limited.

Rather than screening ATRIUM applicants, we take the position that anyone who is willing to address their addictions and their mental health challenges, and has a history of childhood or adult-onset abuse, is appropriate for ATRIUM work. We don't screen out people who have a diagnosis of serious mental illness, who are actively engaged in addictive behaviors, or who don't have an individual counselor or therapist. Instead, we use the intake meeting to develop a couple of simple guidelines for participation in the group:

1. To avoid disruptive or nonproductive group activity, participants should not attend a session while they are actively using their addiction—they are asked not to come to a group while they are high or in the midst of a cutting episode or a binge-purge episode.
2. We ask people what they anticipate needing from us to help them get the most out of being in the group. If they tend to be very quiet or can't stop talking, how can we help them regulate their participation? Or if someone knows that she is likely to dissociate when triggered by certain words or topics, we might ask what works best to help her come back into being present.

When giving potential ATRIUM participants a preview of the work we'll be doing, we have the opportunity to emphasize that while we will connect the impact of each person's trauma with current problems, we will work primarily to give people new coping tools rather than delve into the details of past abuse.

Disclosure Issues

The disclosure of emotionally intense, potentially triggering details of a traumatic experience is a complex challenge. For a long time, disclosure of childhood abuse (and adult violence) had been prohibited by family members, mental health professionals, and society. Over the past two decades, the pendulum has swung towards disclosure, sometimes to the point of endangering the survivor (as in disclosing a painful trauma history on talk shows). Now, there is a backlash which threatens to once again silence the trauma survivor—possible accusations of False Memory Syndrome frighten therapists who do not want to be legally accused of leading survivors into recounting incidents of earlier abuse that the perpetrator or the survivor's family claims never happened.

We honor the telling of one's trauma story to sympathetic, supportive listeners, and we think that if every survivor could do so, Trauma Reenactment would not be so prevalent. But we have also learned from both our personal and professional experience that simply retelling the traumatic past can trigger self-harm unless new coping skills are offered and the profound experience of old isolation and nonprotection is replaced with the experience of connectedness. It is for these reasons that we explain during the intake that the ATRIUM sessions will not be primarily concerned with the retelling of the trauma story.

Also during the intake meeting, we explain for the first time something that we will repeat many more times in the group: Trauma Reenactment does not mean that women will literally enact something in the group that is part of their trauma story—this is not a psychodrama group for the dramatic reenactment of trauma. If this isn't clearly stated, some women will spend time fearing that they will be called upon to act out a rendition of their abuse for the group.

Attendance and Attrition

If you are an ATRIUM facilitator, you need to find a balance between enthusiasm and realism. You need to be realistic about the lives of the people for whom the model has been created. People with addictions and trauma have predictable challenges every day, including compromised physical health, economic stress, childcare problems, turbulent relationships, and internal struggles spanning a broad spectrum. All of the above, coupled with the addictions themselves, may contribute to a pattern of erratic attendance at all help-providing opportunities, including ATRIUM sessions. With this reality in mind, we have designed the ATRIUM protocol so that people can benefit even if they can't attend every session. We suggest that ATRIUM facilitators anticipate sporadic absenteeism and be prepared for a number of drop-outs. Even when women show up regularly for sessions, they may have a difficult time remaining in the session for the entire 90 minutes, due to the combination of addiction- and mental health–based restlessness and the general life stressors competing with their efforts in recovery. For people who are very anxious or frequently dissociate, it is often quite challenging to remain present throughout an entire 90-minute session. We suggest that you remind participants who have trouble staying present that they use the skills they are learning in ATRIUM (i.e., breathing, deep muscle relaxation, and controlled visualization).

However, the facilitators can and should remain enthusiastic and hopeful. Remind ATRIUM participants that they will get the most from the program if they try to attend all 12 sessions, return to the group sessions even if they have missed a meeting, and remain in the room for the entire 90 minutes of the session.

Respecting Boundaries

We think it is very important for time boundaries to be precisely maintained. For people whose lives are chaotic, knowing that the sessions will begin and end on time is very helpful. These clearly maintained time boundaries also help the ATRIUM facilitators by showing that facilitators are available in a specific role but are not inviting outside-of-session disclosures or in-depth personal support.

Contact with ATRIUM facilitators between sessions is discouraged, except when a participant knows she will be unable to attend a session and calls to leave a message. There are many reasons to limit contact between sessions. Perhaps the most important is to avoid disappointment from a group member when the group leader is unavailable for phone calls or extra "emergency" meetings after previously being accessible. This situation—of abruptly being unavailable after setting up a pattern of generous availability—replicates the early trauma dynamics when the child never knows if she will or won't be comforted, cared for, or protected.

The same dynamics can unfortunately be duplicated by offering unboundaried contact during the 12 weeks of the model and then abruptly ending this contact when the group ends. Instead, ATRIUM participants should be told from the beginning that they will be learning how to become successfully involved in longer-lasting support systems and relationships. When this is the priority throughout the 12-week program, the ending of the group will not be as likely to create an experience of abandonment.

Child Care

We cannot emphasize enough how important it is to have child care available to ATRIUM participants. In our experience of working with women who are coping with addiction and trauma issues, it is the lack of child care more often than any other reason that causes missing sessions or dropping out of the ATRIUM program. These women are often facing extra stressors caused by poverty, a lack of a social network, being cut off from family and friends. For all of these reasons, and because of the challenges of an active addiction, child care is a major problem. Facilitators need to work with the agencies or services sponsoring the ATRIUM program to make sure that arrangements for child care during sessions are made.

Professional and Community Resources

ATRIUM encourages participants to get involved in other forms of support and healing, either concurrent with or subsequent to the 12-week model. ATRIUM prioritizes involvement in any support networks that help participants achieve and maintain a healthy, nonaddictive life. A major goal for ATRIUM facilitators is to help each individual participant explore the best resources for her at this particular time in her life. Some of the most frequently used, compatible resources are the following.

- *12-step programs.* These can be extremely helpful when people feel ready to admit that addiction has made their lives unmanageable and they wish to seek the support of other alcoholics or addicts. Both ATRIUM and 12-step programs work at the mind-body-spirit levels to create change and recovery and view community as a central ingredient of recovery. 12-step groups are accessible to all, free of charge, and exist worldwide. While someone may need to complete the ATRIUM protocol before they fully understand how their addiction is connected to their history of trauma, once they make this connection they will probably need the support of a group that focuses on achieving and maintaining abstinence and a sober lifestyle.

- *Detox and inpatient drug/alcohol rehab services.* When ATRIUM helps someone identify her addiction as a serious problem, she may decide that she needs the support of a detox or rehab facility to achieve abstinence. ATRIUM can give her the knowledge and confidence to collaborate with the detox or rehab staff in making the experience work, instead of being forced into the situation and thus not engaging successfully in the program.

- *Domestic violence and sexual assault services.* Some ATRIUM participants may have currently (or recently) experienced domestic violence or sexual assault. Through participating in ATRIUM, they will hopefully feel empowered to name their abuse and seek related support and counseling. ATRIUM facilitators should have up-to-date information on such services in their local area and help participants make the initial contact.

- *Social and recreational activities.* Social isolation and lack of physical exercise are prevalent issues for people with Trauma Reenactment. We often forget in our helper roles that it is just as important for people with addiction and mental health challenges to be engaged in social or recreational activities as to be receiving symptom-focused services. The ATRIUM approach actively encourages participants to be active socially and recreationally. In the last few sessions of the ATRIUM protocol, getting involved with others in one's community becomes the highest priority. Each individual will find her own preferred groups and activities and facilitators can help her to experiment with various activities and to continue involvement with the groups and activities that she prefers.

- *Trauma therapy.* Some ATRIUM participants may choose to do more intensive work on issues related to interpersonal trauma. ATRIUM facilitators can encourage women to "interview" therapists before committing to a longer-term therapy relationship. You can use the themes of the ATRIUM protocol to help participants develop relevant questions like:
  - "Do you think, in most cases, that a childhood trauma history and a current addiction are related?"
  - "How do you understand the connection between addictions and trauma?"
  - "Do you routinely use hypnotherapy techniques to help people recover repressed childhood memories?" (The answer should be "no.")
  - "Do you have experience in working with people with addictions?"
  - "Do you routinely work with healing the body and spirit as well as the mind? How do you do this?"
- *Other relevant therapies.* DBT (Dialectical Behavior Therapy), a cognitive-behavioral therapy model developed by Marsha Linehan (1993a, 1993b), can be a helpful adjunct to ATRIUM work. Once someone struggling with Trauma Reenactment has learned how her trauma history informs her addiction and mental health challenges and has begun practicing some new skills to help heal mind, body and spirit, she may be ready to learn more in-depth interpersonal skills. DBT is an excellent method for learning more successful ways to interact with others. Like ATRIUM, it assumes that the person has behaved in the only way she could in response to a hostile, invalidating environment, and at the same time that she can learn new skills that will help her feel more connected to others. Unfortunately, DBT must be done with a trained professional so it is not accessible if there are no such professionals in your local area.

EMDR is a technique developed by Francine Shapiro (Shapiro, 1995) that can be helpful to people who need more intensive techniques to regulate their responses to triggering stimuli. Again, we want to emphasize that we do not endorse any hypnotic technique for the retrieval of repressed trauma memories. While we believe trauma survivors should be respected and their memories honored, we do not think it is helpful to force the retrieval of repressed memories through any type of hypnotic technique or suggestion.

How Parents Can Use ATRIUM

Many of the exercises in this book can be used with children. We have found that many mothers are very excited about teaching their children the same self-care exercises they are learning for themselves. Depending on the child's age, the exercises for breathing, muscle relaxation, and other body-based coping skills can easily be taught. These exercises can be very helpful with stressful parenting dynamics and to enrich how parents and their children can share in the recovery experience. Some mothers have also found it very helpful to share didactic components with their children, especially when the children have also been abused and are struggling with the repercussions in their own patterns of trauma reenactment.

Using the Manual

The following chapters will provide detailed direction for each of the 12 sessions of the ATRIUM model. This manual includes exercises and handouts that can be used for both group sessions directed by group leaders, and by individuals on their own (or by group members or individual clients between sessions). There are nonacademic discussions about why trauma and addictions often co-occur, how to understand the challenges of recovery, and how to communicate to others what it is like to struggle with the symptoms of both addiction and trauma.

We urge facilitators to follow the guidelines, instructions, process, and experiential exercises, and we have also learned that sometimes it is necessary to change the order of exercises, to change the wording of instructions, and to even occasionally omit something—particularly from the didactic component. We also encourage group leaders to figure out how long you want to spend on each component; if you are co-leading a group, help each other to stay with the planned schedule. While you may feel pressured to fit all the components into each session or feel uncomfortable ending discussions, we believe that this very structured and instructional way of working is the most useful and safest way to help people with Trauma Reenactment histories begin a more successful recovery experience.

The last section of the manual gives the user ideas about ways to become more engaged in a variety of helping resources and urges ATRIUM graduates to get active in helping others, which is the last stage of the recovery process. We think that the ATRIUM protocol is a good beginning, but that the path to recovery is a long and rich journey. We wish everyone a safe and healing trip on the road they are about to travel!

PART II
The Outer Circle

First Steps
to Creating Safety:
Outside and In

Overview for Group Leaders

Session I is based upon the ideas central to the Outer Circle, which focuses on creating safety and building a supportive group environment within which members can feel comfortable listening, sharing, and actively engaging with the group topics. Creating the group guidelines collaboratively fosters group unity and empowers the members to be responsible for establishing their own healthy and supportive boundaries.

This session also begins the process of cultivating within each group member the ability to create safety *within* oneself. Information on the basic principles of the **traumatic stress response** is presented in order to provide participants with a framework for understanding their own body-mind-spirit–based response to early trauma. A group discussion of the ways in which traumatic stress shows up in the lives of the participants helps to concretely link the session topic to the members' lived experience. It also allows for the exploration of old messages about and current responses to the effects of traumatic stress (i.e., old messages like "It's all in your head" and effective but destructive responses like alcohol and/or substance abuse).

Introducing the fundamentals of the **relaxation response** serves several purposes. First, training in diaphragmatic breathing establishes the foundation upon which many relaxation exercises are built. The practice of relaxation techniques, including mindfulness meditation, visualization, and deep muscle relaxation training is an important component that will be used frequently over the 12 weeks of the group. Second, these techniques can help individuals learn how to better manage the effects of traumatic stress. Relaxation training

47

works to stabilize dysregulation of the body-mind-spirit (**3-D distress**) by help-ing group members develop internal sources of self-soothing and comfort in order to replace external ones like alcohol and drugs. Third, by introducing diaphragmatic breathing early in the treatment process, participants are *imme-diately* provided with an alternative to addictive behavior in their efforts to cope with their physical, emotional, and spiritual pain.

Providing structure and guiding the development of ground rules helps demonstrate to members ways of creating safety for themselves within an exter-nal environment. Information regarding traumatic stress and a discussion of its personal impact demystifies the complex effects of trauma, while training in relaxation techniques enhances the capacity for adaptive self-soothing. These aspects of session 1 can help participants begin the process of establishing a sense of safety within themselves, within their own internal environment. A solid foun-dation for proactive self-healing within a safe, responsive, and collaboratively cre-ated setting is thus established. This preliminary and introductory groundwork sets the stage for the remainder of the work to be done in sessions 2–12.

Group Leaders' Tasks for Session 1

Group leaders should facilitate the following group processes:

- Introduction: introduction among group members and facilitators, review-ing the purpose of the group, creating safety within the group.
- Didactic Component: identification of the basic principles of the traumatic stress response.
- Experiential Component: introduction to the relaxation response.
- Process Component: exploration of the relationship between traumatic stress and addiction.
- Maintenance: developing a daily practice of self-care.

Group Leaders' Pre-Group Preparation for Session 1

1. Read through the entire session to familiarize yourself with the topics and review any unfamiliar or uncertain areas. (Do this each week!)
2. Begin your own relaxation response training prior to the start of group.
3. Participant handouts can be found at the end of this manual. Copies should be made ahead of time and distributed to group members as the session begins.
4. Anticipate and be prepared to help participants who have difficulty with the relaxation response training.

Group Member Goals for Session 1

Group members should achieve the following goals:

- identify how the traumatic stress response presents itself along mind-body-spirit dimensions
- receive introductory training in the relaxation response
- gain an understanding of the role their addiction plays in mediating the traumatic stress response

■Introduction

Creating Safety within the Group

A brief explanation of the purpose of the treatment group should be presented. Although this will have already occurred in the screening process, a brief review with the entire group present helps assure that everyone is clear about the focus and direction of the group.

Purpose of the Group

Step 1: Ask participants to briefly say who they are (leaders should begin with their own introductions).

Step 2: Ask participants what they think the purpose of the group is.

Step 3: Validate and clarify their understanding by stating a version of the following: *"This 12-week group is designed to help you gain insight and skills in order to better manage the difficult experience of dealing with the effects of trauma and addictions in your life. Traumatic experiences can cause 3-D distress, or distress in the body, the mind, and the spirit. As a result, many people use alcohol, drugs, food, and other forms of addiction to ease their pain. However, these self-destructive behaviors only serve to recreate the self-destruction of early abuse. This group will help you discover ways to stop the self-destructive cycle of Trauma Reenactment."*

Ground Rules

Basic guidelines for group participation and confidentiality, should be identified. Defining the ground rules right from the start serves to create a safe group "culture" within which group members can feel comfortable talking about their feelings, asking questions, and engaging actively with the material presented.

Suggested Ground Rules

1. Group members should honor each other's confidentiality—what is said in the group should stay in the group.
2. Group members should contact group leaders if they are unable to attend a session.
3. Group members will respect all opinions expressed in the group.
4. Contact between group members outside of group meetings is permitted.
5. Be aware of everyone's need to talk and share time accordingly.
6. Do not come to group under the influence of alcohol or drugs.

HELPFUL HINTS

Keep the ground rules short, simple, and direct.

Guidelines, in addition to the ones suggested, should be generated by the group members.

Do the best you can to obtain a group consensus.

Confidentiality is one ground rule that should be non-negotiable.

■ Didactic Component

Basic Principles of the Traumatic Stress Response

Although the traumatic stress response is a complex physiological response, it can be presented in easily understandable terms. Use the following guidelines and the handouts at the end of the manual to present the fundamental ideas behind the traumatic stress response.

HELPFUL HINTS

Have group members follow along with the handouts provided for session 1.

Reassure participants that all concepts and ideas covered each week will be revisited.

The Fight or Flight Response

What we know about the traumatic stress response is based upon what we know about the universal response to stress or threat called the **fight or flight response**, which we all have within us. When we perceive ourselves to be in a dangerous or threatening situation, a part of the brain (called the amygdala) signals the rest of the body to go on alert status. As a result of this signal, numerous physiological responses occur which can include an increase in heart rate, blood pressure, and muscle tension; blood being shunted away from the periphery of the body; dilation of the eyes; shallow breathing; tunnel vision; and the release of chemicals called catecholomines (i.e., norepinephrine, epinephrine, and dopamine) from the brain into the body.

A Normal Response

This fight or flight response is normal and is observed in all kinds of animals besides humans. In most cases, when the danger or threat has passed, the body returns to its normal state. Heart rate and blood pressure decrease; muscular tension is released; blood flow, vision, and breathing return to normal; and the flood of stress hormones subsides. The fight or flight response is an adaptive response that enables us and other animals to prepare to respond to perceived threats in the most efficient and most life-preserving manner: by fighting the threat or fleeing the threat. This highly aroused state helps us protect ourselves from harm in the immediate presence of danger.

What Goes Wrong

For many people who have had chronic and/or overwhelming experiences of trauma (situations in which the perceived threat of danger rarely subsides or the fearful experience overwhelms an individual's capacity to make sense of the event), the mechanism and process which regulates the fight or flight response can become chronically dysregulated. This regulatory mechanism may begin to function poorly, erratically, or not at all. As a result, some trauma survivors may become oversensitized and respond to normal or mildly threatening events in a heightened manner. Others may "shut down" or "numb out" in the face of less threatening experiences. Still others may respond to memories of the traumatic event with a full flight or fight response as if the trauma was reoccurring in that moment. When these dysregulated responses occur over and over again, this process can become almost automatic and embedded within the response system of the body. This response has been identified as the **traumatic stress response**.

Effects of the Traumatic Stress Response

Some common experiences linked to the effects of the traumatic stress response include the following:

Body	Mind	Spirit
addiction	addiction	addiction
self-harming behavior	flashbacks	alienation
heightened startle response	depression	loss of faith

physical pain including:
    fibromyalgia
    GI pain
    pelvic pain
	dissociation
	tearfulness
	inability to cry
	anxiety
		isolation
		loss of purpose
		loss of meaning
		loss of hope

muscle tension	learned helplessness	apathy
eating disorders	negative thinking	self-degradation

■ Experiential Component

Introduction to the Relaxation Response

Use the following instructions to teach participants the basics of diaphragmatic breathing. As a group facilitator, you should also practice relaxation techniques. The exercise should take approximately 10 minutes.

Introduction

"When you watch a newborn baby breathe, you may notice that its belly rises and falls, swelling and deflating like a little balloon. Under stress, our breathing changes. Chronic or overwhelming acute stress can alter our breathing pattern on a long-term basis. The relaxation response was developed to help people learn to breathe more fully and deeply and thereby return to a more natural cycle of breathing. Deep breathing on a regular basis can provide a kind of 'antidote' to the hyperarousal that can result from trauma. The relaxation response is an effective alternative to substance abuse and other forms of self-harming responses. A regular practice of relaxation techniques like the relaxation response and other methods can help the dysfunctional arousal system to improve and even regain healthy function."

HELPFUL HINTS

You may want to use soft, soothing background music for this exercise.

Because of the effects of traumatic stress, some survivors may have a great deal of difficulty initially with relaxation exercises. You should be prepared to address these concerns. Inform participants that the relaxation response may be difficult at first but that with continued practice, it will become easier.

Encourage participants to move at their own pace. If breathing more deeply begins to become uncomfortable, have them breathe as deeply as they can without discomfort. As they become accustomed to breathing more deeply, they will increase the depth of their breathing cycle over time.

Ask group members who feel increased anxiety when they close their eyes or focus internally to focus externally instead.

Participants can also say a word or a phrase to themselves as they inhale and exhale. Some suggestions include "peace," "breathe," "relax," "release," or simply counting from 1 to 10 over and over. Also, individuals can visualize and say to themselves "I breathe in light and energy, I breathe out tension and stress."

Guide participants to stay with the exercise for as long as they can—it will get better with time and practice!

Invite participants to log their experience of the exercise over time so they can monitor their improvement.

This critical exercise provides the foundation for many experiential exercises to follow. Take the time necessary to make sure members understand both the importance of the relaxation response as well as how to proceed safely.

Instructions

Step 1. *"Make yourselves comfortable in your chairs. Uncross your arms and legs and allow yourself to settle into the chair."*

Step 2. *"If you feel comfortable doing so, close your eyes. If this is uncomfortable for you, keep your eyes open and allow your gaze to fall forward and down toward the floor in a soft focus."*

Step 3. *"Begin to allow your focus to turn inward. Tune in to the pattern of your breath. Without making any changes just yet, simply notice your breath. . . . What moves when you breathe?. . . How does it feel as the air passes into and out of your body?"*

Step 4. *"Now begin to allow your breath to move in through the nostrils and out through your mouth as your breath becomes deeper and slower . . . breathing deeply in and deeply out . . . allow yourself to become more and more relaxed with each breath . . . allow yourself to put your worries and concerns aside for just a little while . . . allow yourself the gift of this time to be still and calm."*

Step 5. *"You may notice that your mind begins to wander or that you become distracted. This is normal. When you find your mind wandering, just notice that it is wandering and gently, without making any judgments of right or wrong, just bring your attention back to your breath. . . ."*

Step 6. *"Allow yourself to release any tension you may be holding in your body as you exhale. . . . Imagine that you are breathing in light and energy and exhaling tensions and worry."*

Step 7. Allow group members to continue their diaphragmatic exercises on their own for a minute or two.

Step 8. *"Continue to breathe deeply and slowly. . . . When you are ready, begin to allow your breathing to return to normal and your focus to return to your surroundings. . . . Very gently, you begin to feel your body in the chair. . . . You may want to begin to gently move your hands and feet. . . . At your own pace—take your time, there is no need to rush—bring yourself slowly and gently back into your surroundings and when you are ready, please open your eyes."*

After the exercise is over, allow the members a few minutes to talk about their experience. Reassure them that it may take some practice for this exercise to bring some relief and invite them to try the exercise twice daily for a few minutes over the next week.

HELPFUL HINTS

Encourage the participation of all group members. Be careful not to force more withdrawn individuals to speak if they are not ready. Set appropriate limits with members who may want to dominate the group. *Do* consistently and supportively offer everyone an invitation to participate.

Monitor the group for signs that any participant is beginning to experience acute distress. Intervene only when an individual's distress significantly disrupts the group.

■Process Component

How Does Traumatic Stress Show up for You?

Invite group members to engage with the following questions (encourage them to respond along the dimensions of body-mind-spirit). This process discussion will help the participants identify how the traumatic stress response is present in their own lives.

- How has traumatic stress shown up in your body?
- How has traumatic stress affected your mind, thoughts, and feelings?
- How has traumatic stress affected your spirit?

- What were the stories you told yourself or that others told you to explain these experiences? (i.e. "It's all in your head," "It can't be that bad," "Be tough," "You're making yourself sick," etc.)
- How has your addiction helped or hindered these experiences?
- In what ways has your experience with traumatic stress *positively* impacted your mind, body and spirit by helping you to develop positive ways of coping with difficulty?

Maintenance

Practice Makes "Better"

This final section helps lay the groundwork for long-term maintenance of the changes made during group. Offer the following to encourage healthy patterns of enduring change.

"You have been carrying 3-D distress with you for a very long time. And over time you have developed a number of ways—some healthy, some not—to help manage your 3-D distress. In order to undo the effects, it will take time, patience, and the consistent practice of the techniques you learn here. Consider making these relaxation techniques a regular practice or daily discipline that will help you have the life you want and deserve. Just like many other things we do to care for ourselves, this practice can become a new way of caring for yourself. With intention, plan daily when and where you will practice the different techniques you will be learning."

Understanding Trauma Reenactment

Overview for Group Leaders

Session 2 is designed to explain Trauma Reenactment and to explore how this process has presented itself in, and often dominated the lives of, the group members. Focus on the Outer Circle continues as participants identify dominant self-narratives (or the primary stories and meanings they have arrived at) regarding their abuse. The safety of the group setting should deepen as members also begin to understand how their early family experiences have contributed to their current distress and how their early trauma plays out and has power in their own lives even now.

Trauma Reenactment is a way of understanding how individuals who have been abused and suffered trauma attempt to come to terms with, make meaning of, and transform these difficult experiences. In an effort to regain one's balance following trauma and abuse, an individual may actually recreate the experience in both literal and symbolic ways. Although this seems strange, it is quite common. As living, thinking organisms, we human beings are continuously making sense of the events around us. We are instantaneously processing information, categorizing it, labeling it, and then putting it where it belongs—in our "meaning-making" bin! However, when an event so overwhelms our body, mind, and spirit (there's that 3-D distress again!) and fails to fit into our "meaning-making" bin, we become engaged in an ongoing cycle of trying to regain our balance by reenacting the event over and over. It is almost as if the trauma has become stuck in our psyche and we rework it, relive it, and replay it in often automatic and unconscious ways. The destructive process of abuse is carried forward and translated into current self-destructive behaviors that more often than not reflect the earlier trauma in a significant way.

An introduction to the idea of the **Triadic Self** in this session will provide a useful framework for understanding what gets reenacted and played out in the lives of the group members and will set the groundwork for the next session on addictions and trauma. This central concept explains how participants have internalized or taken in the triadic relationship of the original trauma in order to make the event fit into their "meaning-making" bins as best they can. Survivors of trauma often take in and take on the relational (or interactive) roles of the **Abuser,** the **Victim,** and the **Nonprotecting Bystander** from the original trauma. Enacting the role of the Abuser, the individual may engage in self-destructive behavior; as the Victim, she may feel frightened and ashamed; as the Nonprotecting Bystander, she may feel helpless and unable to stop the destructive behavior. For each group member, the actual Abuser and Nonprotecting Bystander roles will be different but each has in some way taken in the triadic relationship of the original abuse and have become transformed. Identifying and then challenging the dominant messages that have been internalized by adopting these roles will help participants begin the process of proactively recreating their lived experience from a place of empowerment and resilience.

Group Leaders' Tasks for Session 2

Group leaders should facilitate the following group processes:

- Guided Relaxation and Check-In: facilitate relaxation exercise and lead a brief review of the past week and the relaxation response homework assignment.
- Didactic Component: information provided on Trauma Reenactment (TR).
- Process Component: identification of Triadic Self and how the roles manifest for members.
- Experiential Component: identification of and challenges to self-destructive messages.
- Maintenance: creating serenity and reflection.

Group Leaders' Pre-Group Preparation for Session 2

1. Obtain soothing music to play for the beginning of group and during the relaxation exercise.
2. Purchase post-its for the experiential component.

3. Have a space at the front of the group room (a wall, blackboard, or free-standing tripod) where group members can stick the post-its during the experiential exercise.

Group Member Goals for Session 2

Group members should achieve the following goals:

- understand the basic idea of Trauma Reenactment
- identify how Trauma Reenactment plays out in their own lives and in their own behavior
- identify the three "selves" of the Triadic Self
- identify and challenge some of the destructive "self-talk" that can contribute to self-harming behaviors

■Guided Relaxation Exercise and Check-In

HELPFUL HINTS

You may want to have quiet music playing as participants enter the group room. Invite them to begin the relaxation response as they await the arrival of other group members.

Important: Take the time necessary during this session to establish the expectation that group members will practice their relaxation exercises during the week. If participants are struggling, take the time to problem solve and address barriers to their participating in this *fundamental* and *essential* part of treatment. Inform the group that progress regarding these exercises and their application will be reviewed each week until each group member has established a consistent relaxation practice.

Keep the check-in brief and focused as there is a great deal of material and key concepts to cover in this session.

At the start of the session each week, facilitators should lead participants in a brief relaxation response exercise. Each week, one minute will be added on to the length of time spent on the relaxation exercise. So for session 2 the group will practice diaphragmatic breathing for two minutes; for session 3 facilitators should lead the group in the relaxation response for three minutes, and so on. In addition, members should have an opportunity to check-in. After the relaxation exercise, invite all participants to briefly address the following questions:

→ In a few words, tell us how your relaxation practice went this past week?

→ Last week we talked about traumatic stress. Did you have any insights or reflections over the past week that you would like to share about that?

■Didactic Component

Understanding Trauma Reenactment (TR)

As noted earlier, Trauma Reenactment (TR) is a way many people make sense of overwhelming experiences of trauma and abuse. It is important to have group members understand that TR is an adaptive response to trauma, an effort to manage the unmanageable. The following **Recipe for TR** can be used, along with the handouts at the end of the manual, to help explain what TR is.

The Results.   As a result of overwhelming trauma, an individual is often forced to process the abuse in a way that can significantly impact and shape who they are physically, mentally, and spiritually. In an effort to manage and make sense of the baked-in thoughts, feelings, and behaviors linked to the experience of abuse and to soothe the flames of intolerable trauma, an individual may recreate the recipe for themselves over and over again. The recipe then becomes one's standard fare or the usual way of responding to a wide range of stressful experiences.

What is Trauma Reenactment?

Trauma Reenactment occurs when trauma and abuse from the past is carried forward into your life today and is reenacted by self-destructive behaviors that either symbolically or literally represent the trauma of the past.

Recipe for Trauma Reenactment (TR)

1. Take one person (either a child or an adult).
2. Place them in an environment where they either cannot get help or access to help is difficult to obtain.
3. Pour abusive experiences in overwhelming portions on them. These experiences can entail emotional, physical, sexual abuse, and neglect, or any combination of the above. The amount of trauma needed to produce TR will vary as what is overwhelming is individually determined. Some individuals will develop TR to singular or limited experiences of trauma while others will develop TR in response to chronic long-term abuse.
4. Once the trauma and abuse has completely coated and saturated the individual, you might add to the mix by threatening them, denying what happened, saying that what has happened was "not that bad," or saying that the abuse was their own fault.

Behaviors that can be seen as reenactments of past abuse include, but are not limited to:

alcohol abuse/dependence	drug abuse/dependence
cutting oneself	being in abusive relationships
burning oneself	somatic complaints
bingeing on food	putting oneself in dangerous situations
purging/vomiting	abusing others
hitting/striking oneself	loss of spirituality/faith
self-degrading, negative thoughts	self-neglect
obsessing about suicide	setting oneself up for failure

sexual activity that you don't feel good about

sexual partners that you don't feel good about

These reenacting behaviors, thoughts, and feelings are a survivor's best efforts at regaining the balance they lost as a result of overwhelming trauma.

■Process Component

Invite group members to explore the following questions that are designed to help them identify their own patterns of Trauma Reenactment. Ask group members to work alone with their session 2 handout for a few minutes. Once again, encourage them to respond along body-mind-spirit dimensions.

HELPFUL HINTS

It is not necessary for participants to disclose the specifics of their abuse in order to participate in this exercise (or for that matter, in this group treatment). Some members may disclose over time, others may not. At this early juncture, before safety is established and before participants can soothe themselves in alternative ways, full disclosure is discouraged. Gently redirect participants who may feel pressure to prematurely disclose extensive details of their early abuse or trauma.

Check to make sure that everyone who wanted to share had the opportunity to do so.

- How have you physically reenacted your own experience of trauma? (*Sample responses:* engaging in self-mutilating behavior such as cutting, burning oneself, ignoring signs of fatigue or pain, abusing substances and losing control of oneself, bingeing and/or purging, placing oneself in physical danger, abusing/neglecting others, etc.)

- How have you emotionally and mentally recreated your early experience of abuse? (*Sample responses:* abusing substances in order to be numb or over-stimulate oneself cognitively, setting oneself up to feel shame or guilt, sabotaging attempts at success, denying or minimizing the effects of trauma on one's life, having negative thoughts about one's self-worth, etc.)

- How has your early trauma played out along spiritual dimensions? (*Sample responses:* a disconnection from God or a religious community, isolation and despair, narrowed or eliminated the possibility of believing in a higher power or in such things as love and hope, etc.)

- In what ways has your experience of trauma led to positive reexperiences along the mind-body-spirit dimension? (*Sample responses:* forced me to develop physical strength, tolerance, acceptance, fostered within me a deep sense of caring for children, made me pay more attention to my feelings and thoughts, made me more sensitive to the suffering of others, etc.)

HELPFUL HINT

Have participants follow along with the illustration on the hand-out sheet.

■Experiential Component

Introduction to the Triadic Self

Group facilitators will need to offer an explanation of the Triadic Self in order to present this exercise. A brief overview is all that is needed here as the Triadic Self will be reviewed again in session 3 and is woven into the remainder of the group process.

What is being reenacted in Trauma Reenactment?
The relationship between yourself (Victim), the perpetrator of the trauma (Abuser), and anyone in your life at the time who had the power to stop the abuse but did not (Nonprotecting Bystander).

How does this happen?
① Individuals who experience trauma and abuse may internalize this 3-way (or triadic) abusive relationship. ② This internalization results in the development of the Triadic Self (which includes the victim-self, the abuser-self, and the nonprotecting bystander–self). ③ After taking in this triadic abusive relationship, the individual then reenacts the abusive relationship dynamics over and over again.

Experiential Exercise

The following exercise will help group members under-stand the influence of the Triadic Self. It will also begin to allow participants to identify and challenge the negative thoughts that are rooted in the abusive Triadic Self and that contribute to the cycle of Trauma Reenactment. The essential purpose of this exercise is to assist group members in changing the destructive messages they are send-ing themselves as a result of their early abuse and the subsequent internalization of the Triadic Self . . . to begin to have participants send messages to themselves as if they were someone they care about!

> **HELPFUL HINT**
> Be prepared to help group members develop positive and affirming responses or challenges to the negative thoughts and messages rooted in the Triadic Self.

1. Provide group members with the handout entitled "Messages from and to the Triadic Self." (This handout looks like a bulletin board divided into three sections, front and back with an assortment of blank memo notes spread across it.) Also, provide each participant with post-its.

2. On the side that says "Messages from. . . ." invite participants to take ten minutes to fill in the appropriate sections (abuser-self, victim-self, non-protecting bystander–self), with the messages they continue to hear or tell themselves that come from these internalized negative sources. For example, under abuser-self, participants may write, "You are no good," "I am going to hurt you," "This is your fault," etc. *If the abuser was "kind" and nonthreatening, be sure that the group member is able to communicate the message of distrust and abuse of power that is a part of these types of abu-sive relationships.* Under victim-self, participants may write things like "I am scared," "I hate this," "I am all alone," " I deserve this," "I hate myself," etc. Under nonprotecting bystander–self, participants may write things like "I can't protect you," "I can't stop this," " I am not strong enough to handle this," "I don't see anything wrong," "You're making this up," etc.

3. After ten minutes, allow members to share what the exercise was like and ask if anyone was surprised by what they wrote. Participants can share what they wrote with the rest of the group by writing some of these mes-sages on post-its, placing them on the wall or blackboard at the front of the room, and having group members read them aloud.

4. On the opposite side of the sheet, it should read "Messages to. . . ." This time encourage participants to respond to the negative messages they just identified in ways that challenge the truth of the negative statements or in ways that bring them comfort and lead to positive feelings. For example,

under the message to the abuser-self, members may write, "You are lying when you say I am no good" (challenging the truth of the statement "You are no good"), "I will not let you hurt me anymore" (expressing self-power and strength in response to the threat of harm), "This is not my fault and I have done nothing wrong" (comforting and challenging in response to the message "This is your fault"). *In response to a nonthreatening abuser, one may write the message "You do not love me and I do not trust you."*

Under victim-self, participants may respond by writing things like "I know you are scared but he/she can't hurt you anymore," "I know this is awful, but hold on, it will get better," "I know you feel alone right now, but I care about you," "You have done nothing to deserve this," "You are feeling bad about yourself right now and hating yourself but I know you have nothing to be ashamed of," etc.

Under nonprotecting bystander–self, group members may respond with "You couldn't protect me then, but I will protect myself now," "I can stop this cycle of abuse!" "I will become strong enough to handle this," "I know what happened and it was wrong," "The abuse was real," etc.

5. Following this exercise, again take time for members to share their insights and feelings. Allow participants to write "challenge" responses to the negative messages on post-its, place them on a wall or blackboard at the front of the room, and have group members read them aloud. Remember that participants may have trouble at first developing positive and affirming or challenging responses to these internalized negative messages. Be prepared to help individuals identify useful responses and when appropriate, ask other group members for their input.

■Maintenance

As the session ends, share the Serenity Prayer with the group. Explain that it is a prayer or meditation frequently used in Alcoholics Anonymous or Narcotics Anonymous. Encourage members to consider how this prayer applies to what they just learned about their self-destructive behavior patterns.

Serenity Prayer

God (or Higher Power) grant me
the serenity to accept the things I cannot change,
the courage to change the things I can,
and the wisdom to know the difference.

While survivors of abuse have to accept that they cannot change their past experiences of trauma or abuse, they can gain the courage to change the way they respond. Maintaining a position of acceptance on the one hand and change on the other requires the cultivation of wisdom over time. Reflecting on the Serenity Prayer daily is a good way to stay in touch with the ongoing healing process and to remain focused on maintaining positive changes. Invite members to adopt a practice of daily reflecting on the serenity prayer or another verse that speaks to them and empowers their healing process.

Addictions and Trauma Reenactment: Finding Another Way

Overview for Group Leaders

The focus of session 3 is on the specific relationship between addictions and Trauma Reenactment. The Outer Circle themes, including building safety, identifying primary ways of making sense of both addictive behavior and initial trauma, and exploring past experiences of seeking help and validation, continue to guide the group process. Additionally, the group will begin the transition to the Middle Circle as barriers to healing and treatment are examined and alternatives to efforts to soothe and heal themselves are introduced.

The relationship between addictions and Trauma Reenactment is best understood as a paradoxical one. On the one hand, the self-destructive nature of addictions, such as excessive alcohol and drug use, binge eating, sexual compulsivity, etc., can reflect in many ways the devastation of trauma and early abuse. It will be important to emphasize that *how* trauma and early abuse are reenacted will be different for different group members. For example, some individuals who drink may be reenacting the feeling of numbness or recreating the altered state they experienced during their abuse. Some may be using illicit drugs as a way to place themselves in risky circumstances, thus reenacting the danger and fear of the initial trauma. Other group members may use substances or food as a means of recreating the out-of-control feeling that they may have experienced before, during, or after the abuse. Some, as a result of their addiction, will allow and remain in abusive relationships that in turn mirror their early abuse or trauma relationship. Other compulsive self-harming behaviors, such as head banging or cutting or burning oneself, can be seen as direct reflections of the pain of abuse. In any case, the self-destructive cycle of addictions, with shame, fear, anger, and despair at the center, can often be seen as a thinly disguised imitation of the initial experience of trauma and abuse.

On the other hand, addictive behavior is also often rooted in efforts to soothe the 3-D distress that follows in the wake of trauma and abuse. As such, addictive behaviors often represent a repetitive, misguided attempt to return to balance. It is a short-term solution that works. Discomfort and pain in the body can be eased by drugs, alcohol, food, etc. Intense feelings can be numbed or amplified, overwhelming negative thoughts can be drowned out, and the despair of the spirit can be quieted. However, the remedy of drinking, drugging, and other self-destructive addictive behaviors becomes a long-term source of pain. The addiction, then, itself becomes the "abuser." The individual quite literally "takes in" the substance or behavior of choice and the cycle of reenactment begins again.

How does one begin to break through this vicious and destructive cycle? Participants now understand that they have internalized past abusive relationships such that self-destructive behavior has become a dominant way of life. By introducing the concept of the **Protective Presence,** a source of comfort and safety defined by each individual, group members can begin to "take in" self-soothing and self-nurturing images and relationships. The Protective Presence as a new resource for comfort and care can serve to vanquish the abuser-self, provide protection where the nonprotecting bystander–self could not, and surround the victim-self with safety and comfort. Self-harm, then, is replaced by self-care and the self-destructive cycle can begin to end.

Group Leaders' Tasks for Session 3

Group leaders should facilitate the following group processes:

- Guided Relaxation and Check-In: facilitate a brief guided relaxation exercise, check-in with participants regarding their relaxation practice, provide a brief review of Trauma Reenactment and the Triadic Self.
- Didactic Component: present information on the relationship between addictions and Trauma Reenactment.
- Process Component: facilitate reflection and exploration of themes involving addictions as Trauma Reenactment, the cost/benefit ratio of addictive behavior, and barriers to healing and recovery.
- Experiential Component: creating the Protective Presence through the use of music, movement, gesture, and visualization.
- Maintenance: identifying positive sources of comfort, safety, and soothing.

Group Leaders' Pre-Group Preparation for Session 3

1. Prepare music for the Protective Presence experiential exercise. You will need to record the selected piece three times in a row on one tape (see Experiential Component: Creating a Protective Presence on page 80 for more details).

Group Member Goals for Session 3

Group members should achieve the following goals:

- an understanding of the relationship between addictions and Trauma Reenactment
- identify (1) how their own addiction reenacts their own experience of trauma, (2) the cost/benefits of addictive behavior, and (3) barriers to their own healing and recovery
- begin the process of creating internal resources of comfort, security, safety, and soothing

■Guided Relaxation Exercise and Check-In

This week, following a three-minute relaxation exercise, group leaders should check in with participants regarding their ongoing relaxation response practice. Use the following questions as guidelines:

→ How does your body feel now following the relaxation exercise?
→ How often were you able to do your relaxation response practice this past week?
→ How have you found the practice to be helpful or difficult over the past week?

Additionally, facilitators should present a brief overview of Trauma Reenactment and the Triadic Self and encourage the sharing of questions, insights, or reflections that may have arisen over the course of the week. Be sure to emphasize the following central points during the review.

- Trauma Reenactment occurs when trauma and abuse from the past is carried forward into your life today and is reenacted by self-destructive behaviors that either symbolically or literally represent the trauma of the past.

- Trauma Reenactment is an adaptive effort to manage unmanageable 3-D distress.
- Trauma Reenactment manifests differently for different people.
- The Triadic Self represents the internalization of abusive, nonprotecting, victimizing relationships that occurred during the initial trauma or early abuse.

■■Didactic Component

It is important for participants to understand the paradoxical (or seemingly contradictory) relationship between addiction and Trauma Reenactment. But first, facilitators should guide group members in understanding how drinking, drugging, eating, self-injury, etc. represents Trauma Reenactment.

Addictions as Trauma Reenactment

Encourage group members to respond to the following question in a "brainstorming" format and write their answers on the board (answers should be fairly brief and spontaneous).

Note to group members that there are many ways in which the destructive cycle of addiction parallels the destructive cycle of abuse. Invite them to consider other ways that early trauma experiences and abuse are recreated and reenacted through addiction.

Understanding the Paradox

Use the following questions (and the handout for session 3) to help participants understand the paradoxical relationship between addictions and Trauma Reenactment.

What is a paradox? A paradox occurs when two seemingly opposite things are simultaneously true!

How is the relationship between addictions and Trauma Reenactment a paradoxical one? On the one hand, (as we just discovered) excessive and self-destructive addictions can serve to recreate the experience of early abuse or initial trauma on many different levels. On the other hand, an addiction can also serve to provide effective short-term relief from the 3-D distress of trauma.

Why is this important to understand? Because understanding the full nature of addictions—that they serve the dual function of recreating trauma as well as soothing the effects of trauma—can help guide us to finding another way to respond to the trauma we carry inside!

■Process Component

It is also important that group members begin to gain insight into how their own addiction serves as both a source of self-destructive reenactment on one hand and misguided efforts to self-soothe 3-D distress on the other. Encourage participants to use the handouts during this component and to make notes on the sheets provided. Have group members explore the following themes:

1. How does *your* addiction reenact your experience of trauma and/or early abuse?
2. How does your addiction serve to, at least temporarily soothe, your 3-D distress?
3. Attempts to seek treatment and healing represent efforts to find another way to respond to your experience of trauma. In your efforts to deal with your addiction and your experience of trauma, what treatment interventions or self-healing efforts have been helpful and what has not been helpful?

■Experiential Component

Creating a Protective Presence

How do we begin to change the devastating cycle of Trauma Reenactment? Participants demonstrate that they want to find another way to move through their lives by seeking treatment and healing. As such, participants need to begin the process of taking in or internalizing positive, self-nurturing, protective images, connections, and relationships. The Protective

HELPFUL HINTS

Group facilitators should cultivate their own Protective Presence.

Group brainstorming should be done quickly, with almost rapid-fire discussion. Encourage participants to be brief in describing their ideas and images.

Do the Protective Presence exercise with music several times on your own so that transitions will be smooth and fluid.

Presence is introduced here to provide participants with an opportunity to begin to create healthy and self-promoting internal resources of safety, comfort, and soothing. This supportive, nurturing, internalized resource can then serve as a healthy alternative to the paradoxically destructive yet soothing response to the 3-D distress of engaging in addictive behaviors.

Group Brainstorm Question
When you hear the word "protective," what words and images come to mind?

What is the Protective Presence?

The Protective Presence can be thought of as a comforting, soothing, safe, calm resource.

"When you were hurt or traumatized you were unprotected . . . maybe unintentionally, maybe on purpose. In any case, someone did not protect you from your abuser. Experiences like this can leave people feeling unsafe in the world. You might say that in many ways, your addiction(s) to drugs, alcohol, people, food, etc., represents a misguided effort to find protection and safety. (List the images and ideas that the participants identified in the brainstorm exercise and remind them of the "paradox" noted earlier, i.e., addiction as the "abuser" vs. addiction as the "soother.") *The purpose of this exercise is to help you begin to create a positive, self-nurturing, and protective resource of your own that you can call upon in times of 3-D distress. We are going to begin to develop a garden, if you will, of protection, safety . . .* (again, list the words and images participants identified earlier) *for you to live in. And we will begin by planting seeds for the cultivation of an internalized Protective Presence."*

■Group Leaders' Instructions for the Protective Presence Exercise

Step 1. Invite participants to get into comfortable, relaxed, but alert, positions in their seats.

Step 2. Tell them the following:

- *"In just a few minutes, I am going to put on some music. It is very soothing music. We will play this particular piece of music three times."*
- *"The first time we play this music, I simply want you to relax and listen to the music. Please remain seated throughout this exercise."*
- **Alternate method:** If group facilitators feel comfortable doing so, substitute the following for the second part of step 2—*"The first time we play this music, I simply want you to mirror the movements I make. We will remain seated throughout this exercise. The movement that you will be copying from me will be very simple gentle, swaying, gestures—nothing too fancy. I will move very slowly and we will all remain seated throughout the entire exercise."*

Step 3. Continue with the following explanation for when the music plays a second time:

- *"The second time you hear the music I want you to begin to slowly move your hands, arms, torso, etc., on your own. You can move in any way you like. You should seek to create a soothing gesture of your own. I encourage you to experiment freely and unselfconsciously with slow movements. I ask that you remain seated throughout the exercise. Gestures and movement can include many things like holding your own hand, caressing your own cheek, hugging yourself, spreading your arms wide, rocking gently, or it may even mean being still and breathing deeply."*

- *"The movement(s) you choose to use should be one(s) that call(s) forth the images or ideas you noted earlier in the brainstorming session. It should be whatever works best for you (i.e., whatever you find most soothing). You may use the gestures or movements demonstrated by the group leader or those you have created for yourself."*

Step 4. Continue with this explanation for when the music plays a third time:

- *"When you hear the music for the third time, I want those who feel comfortable doing so, to close their eyes. If you are uncomfortable closing your eyes, just let your gaze fall in a soft focus on the floor a foot or two ahead of you."*

- *"I will ask you to move into the most comforting position, movement, and/or gesture that you have discovered. I would like you to maintain this movement throughout the entire song. If you want to change, feel free to do so. But try to stay with what you have found to be most comforting for the duration of the music."*

Step 5. Remind group members of the following:

- *"Don't worry if this sounds a bit confusing. I will lead you through it and direct you in the exercise."*

- *"Breathe deeply and relax throughout the exercise."*

- *"You may feel a bit self-conscious, but stay focused on yourself and on getting the most you can out of this exercise."*

Step 6. Begin the exercise by checking to make sure everyone is in a comfortable position Begin the selected music. Encourage participants to relax and listen to the music. (If the alternate method is used, the group facilitator should begin to move arms and hands very slowly and gently, perhaps rocking the torso rhythmically. Encourage group members to follow your lead and simply copy your movements like a mirror image. Speak softly and in a reassuring tone.)

Step 7. The second time the music plays, invite participants to begin to explore their own comforting movements and gestures. (If the alternate method is used, you may continue to move slowly as well but also encourage group members to discontinue copying you and to create their own movement.) The movements they choose should bring feelings of safety and comfort and soothing to them.

Step 8. The third time the music plays, direct participants to close their eyes. Those who cannot do so should allow their gaze to fall in a soft focus on the floor a foot or two ahead of them. Guide the group members to move into the most comforting pattern they discovered and to gently maintain this movement, gesture, or position throughout the rest of the song. Invite them to allow positive images to emerge as they sustain these soothing movements.

Step 9. As the music fades, encourage participants to allow their focus to return to the group room at their own pace. Direct them to *gently* bring themselves back into the room, to take their time and move at their own pace.

Step 10. Allow time and space for the participants to reflect on and share their experience of this exercise.

■Maintenance

Encourage group members to continue with the ongoing development of a relaxation practice.

"*Seek to create, hold onto, and make use of lasting sources of safety and comfort in your life. Begin by identifying and writing down current positive sources of support, encouragement, safety, and comfort in your life. This can include everything and anything from pets to poems to music to plants and flowers to your sense of spirituality to specific friends, family, etc. Your resources are your resources! Post this list in a visible area of your home and refer to it often when you feel isolated and alone.*"

PART III
The Middle Circle

Finding Emotional Expression and Balance

Overview for Group Leaders

In session 4 the focus of the group narrows in order to examine, explore, and address in more detail the 3-D distress of trauma and early abuse. Themes of the Outer Circle continue to be implicitly relevant in the group process. Concepts central to the Middle Circle, including seeking alternative healing solutions, building support networks, and honoring the impact of trauma while still holding onto hope, move to the foreground. As safety within the group increases and the foundational ideas of the ATRIUM model are introduced, less time is spent on the didactic or information sharing component, and more time is dedicated to the process and experiential components of the group.

In the 3-D model of distress, disruption in any one dimension can negatively affect the other two. In the long-term aftermath of trauma and early abuse, many individuals are left feeling emotionally "off-balance." This disruption of emotion, which is related to the dimension of mind, can serve to increase discomfort in the body and can lead to disconnection from the spirit. *Regulating emotion*, or discovering how to better control that dysregulated emotional thermostat discussed in session 1, can work to help participants regain emotional balance and increase 3-D delight!

The emotional fall-out of trauma has multiple expressions. For some survivors, emotional sensitivity may be heightened while for others the capacity to experience intensity, depth, or range of emotion may be dampened. Still other survivors can experience extreme variability between emotional reactivity and emotional shut-down. Addiction can be seen as an effort to assuage these variable manifestations of emotional discomfort—decreasing reactivity, increasing the capacity for intensity, or evening out the roller coaster of variability. A significant barrier to healing the wounds of trauma and stopping the cycle of Trauma Reenactment is the *short-term* efficacy of drugs and alcohol (or any addictive behavior) in temporarily relieving heightened levels of 3-D distress. Unfortunately, the intense, short-term temporary relief of emotional distress through addiction masks the *longer-term* consequences of self-destructive Trauma Reenactment. It is therefore imperative that participants learn to develop alternatives to their current effective but self-damaging efforts at regaining emotional balance.

Finally, facilitators should note to the group that particularly difficult emotion(s) they struggle with frequently turn out to be one(s) that are an *emotional reenactment of the trauma*. Perhaps it is the rage of the Abuser, the apathy of the Nonprotecting Bystander, or the fear of the Victim that is being played out. Whatever the case, this contextual understanding of out-of-control emotions can help participants make sense of unpredictable and unmanageable feelings and provide them with an opportunity to respond to them in a different, less self-destructive, manner.

Group Leaders' Tasks for Session 4

Group leaders should facilitate the following group processes:

- Guided Relaxation Exercise and Check-In: facilitate relaxation exercise and well-being check-in, along with an update on group members' relaxation response practice, review the Protective Presence and what additional sources of comfort and safety participants have been able to identify over the week.
- Didactic Component: information presented on emotional dysregulation that is secondary to early abuse/trauma and emotional reenactment.
- Process Component: explore questions related to the participant's experience of emotional dysregulation and emotional reenactment as well as how the emotional context of their lives has worked for or against them in their efforts to heal themselves and build connections.
- Experiential Component: identifying unmanageable emotions and how they manifest in mind-body-spirit domains and beginning the process of proactively transforming this experience.
- Maintenance: finding emotional balance through a mindfulness practice.

Group Leaders' Pre-Group Preparation for Session 4

1. Review the emotional pathway section of the didactic component so that you can speak more easily about it.
2. Prepare the posterboard figures for the experiential component in advance (see pages 82 and 83 for more details).

Group Member Goals for Session 4

Group members should achieve the following goals:

- gain a basic understanding of the impact of early trauma and abuse on the emotional system
- examine areas of emotional dysregulation in their own experience, explore how their persistent emotional distress can be understood as emotional reenactment, and identify how their difficult emotions have led to barriers to healing
- experientially explore and work to transform unmanageable, difficult, and destructive negative emotions

▪Guided Relaxation Exercise and Check-In

Following the introductory relaxation exercise (lasting a total of 4 minutes), in this week's check-in, group leaders should allow for an update on participants' ongoing relaxation response practice. Use the following as a guideline:

→ How is your relaxation practice different from when you began a few weeks ago?

Before the next check-in question, group leaders should present a brief review of the Protective Presence and explore how group members have begun to bring this resource into their live. The following can serve as a helpful guide for this brief review:

- The *Protective Presence* can be thought of as a comforting, soothing, safe, calm resource (*list the qualities, images, and ideas generated by the group in session 3*).
- The *Protective Presence* can begin to serve as a replacement for self-destructive efforts at self-soothing like drinking, drugging, binge-eating, etc.

- The *Protective Presence* can be powerful enough to overcome the Abuser inside.

Following this review, ask participants to respond to the following question:

→ What did you do this week to cultivate a Protective Presence in your life?

HELPFUL HINTS

Direct participants to use the handout to follow along with this discussion.

It is important to emphasize that different people will have different emotional experiences in response to their trauma.

■ Didactic Component

The Impact of Traumatic Stress on the Emotional System

The following information will help reinforce central ideas regarding traumatic stress and aid participants in understanding how their emotional system may have become disrupted during their abuse or early trauma. It will also help participants to grasp the idea of emotional reenactment.

Pathway to Emotional Dysregulation and Emotional Reenactment (Or How We Lose Our Emotional Balance as a Result of Trauma)

As an individual encounters *overwhelming trauma or abuse*, information about this experience is perceived through the senses and processed by the brain . . .

The **amygdala** is the part of the brain that functions as an emotional scanner, informing us about the emotional significance of an event. It also acts as an early warning alarm system . . .

When an individual is in a situation in which they perceive threat, it is the amygdala that sounds the alarm and kick starts the **fight or flight response** . . .

The emotional amygdala sounds this alarm *before* the more slowly triggered **neocortex** (or that part of the brain which helps us identify, organize, and fully process information) has a chance to respond to the threat . . .

↓

When the threat passes, functioning returns to homeostasis or *balance* and the neocortex can then make more sense of the experience . . .

↓

But when the regulatory system is *overwhelmed* by the traumatic event, its functioning can become *disrupted* . . .

↓

During a traumatic event, thinking (which helps mediate, make sense of, and assuage or soothe emotion) gets bypassed. As a result, individuals may fail to fully process the traumatic event. The unprocessed, fragmented, and *emotionally charged bits* of the trauma (including body response, feelings, and meaning of the event) can become stored in memory with no clear narrative or personal interpretation to help make the experience make sense . . .

↓

Because of this *sloppy* storage of unprocessed emotional material, things that happen today may trigger emotional responses associated with the past trauma . . .

↓

A pattern of *emotional reenactment* (or recreating, reliving, reexperiencing emotions associated with the trauma) can get set into motion . . .

↓

Leaving one continually struggling for *emotional balance* . . .

Why Is This Important?

"*It is important to understand why trauma can leave us emotionally off-balance because feelings and emotions connect us to ourselves, to others, and to our spirituality. When emotional functioning is disrupted, unpredictable, and unmanageable, it is reflected in our lives; our relationship to ourselves, others, and our spirituality becomes disrupted, unpredictable, and unmanageable.*

"*It is also important to understand that many of the emotions we struggle with in our lives today are emotional reenactments of the early abuse or trauma of the past. The undigested or frozen feelings of the Victim (such as fear, despair, confusion, etc.), the Abuser (such as rage, desire for power or control, disgust, etc.), and the Nonprotecting Bystander (apathy, uncertainty, passivity, shame, helplessness, etc.) may play out repeatedly. Addictions are then utilized to both soothe and further perpetuate the destructive reenactment cycle.*"

■ Experiential Component

Transforming the Experience of Difficult Feelings: from 3-D Distress to 3-D Delight! (Or at Least to "3-D De-Calm"!)

The painful feelings associated with emotional reenactment are frequently experienced as intolerable. Remove the one effective source of emotional comfort, no matter how self-destructive, and you leave an individual unprotected and undefended against a potential flood of overwhelming and difficult feelings—intense emotions that may have been held at bay or regulated by alcohol, drugs, and other addictions. The following experiential exercise is designed to help group members first identify these kinds of unmanageable emotions and then to explore how they manifest in 3-D distress in the mind-body-spirit. The ultimate goal is to give participants an experiential tool or technique to utilize in expressing and transforming difficult feelings.

HELPFUL HINTS

Prepare posterboard figures in advance using model below.

Figures should be between 12 to 18 inches in size.

You might want to play soothing, calming music as individuals work on these exercises.

The idea of this exercise is not to negate or try to eliminate difficult feelings, but to try and empower participants to begin to identify, tolerate, and transform them in their own experience.

■ Group Leaders' Instructions for the 3-D Emotional Expression Exercise

Step 1. Supply participants with a posterboard figure (see below) and crayons, markers, colored pencils, fabric bits, beads, etc.

Step 2. For the first half of the exercise, invite participants to identify a particularly difficult emotion they struggle with and to write and/or draw how this emotion feels in their mind-body-spirit on one side of the posterboard figure. They can draw images, use words, use colors, textures, or any combination of the above. Example:

sAdness
- body feels
  tense
- spirit feels
  broken
- mind feels
  dark + clouded

Step 3. Once participants have completed one side of the figure, guide them to turn it over to the other side and draw and/or write *what they would like these emotions to feel like in their mind-body-spirit*. Encourage them to create soothing, positive, comforting images and to visualize the experience as they craft it on the figure. Example:

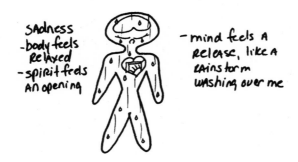

sAdness
- body feels
  Relaxed
- spirit feels
  An opening

- mind feels A
  release, like A
  rainstorm
  washing over me

Step 4. When participants are finished, invite them to share their work with the rest of the group. Guide participants in discussing what the exercise was like for them.

HELPFUL HINT

Remember to encourage the participation of all group members. At this point of the group process, participants should be moving toward deepening trust within the group.

■ Process Component

Use the following questions as guidelines for the process discussion. Encourage participants to identify specific areas of emotional disruption and patterns of emotional reenactment.

1. What have you done in the past to try and address your own emotional disruption?
2. How has your addiction worked to help you regain or try and maintain emotional balance?
3. In what ways is your own emotional disruption an emotional reenactment of your earlier experience of abuse or trauma?

■ Maintenance

Finding Emotional Balance Through a Mindfulness Practice

Participants have hopefully begun a regular relaxation practice. They should be familiar with focusing inward on the breath, noticing and letting go of distracting thoughts, feelings, discomfort in the body, and gently returning their focus to the breath. These same ideas are herein applied to attending to difficult emotional states. Encourage participants to experiment with the following and to consider under what conditions this is a helpful, healthy, adaptive way to manage unmanageable emotions.

- *"Think about your relaxation practice over the past few weeks. One thing that you are learning to do is to pay attention more closely to your breath. You have been practicing tuning in to something that is mostly automatic, unconscious, and taken for granted."*
- *"During your practice, you have learned to notice and then let go of distracting thoughts, feelings, images, and discomfort in your body. You have become both* more mindful *of these things as well as* more able to let them go.*"*
- *"Each time you have noticed these things and then gently, but consistently, returned your focus to your breath, you have made your 'letting-go muscle,' if you will, a little bit stronger."*
- *"As you begin to carry the principles of mindfulness into your life, you may want to begin to apply the same ideas to difficult emotions and feelings."*
- *"In an effort to manage unmanageable feelings in the moment, try and do the following three things:* name them, feel them, *and* let them go.*"*

- *"Naming them allows you to identify and understand your experience. Feeling them allows you to validate your experience. Letting them go, and bringing your focus to positive thoughts and comforting images, helps you manage unmanageable feelings that may lead you to engage in self-destructive Trauma Reenacting–behaviors like drinking, drugging, self-harming, and other self-destructive behaviors."*

- *"Just like the development of any other skill (piano, skiing, whatever!), this takes practice over time. Begin practicing now and you will be that much farther along."*

Managing Dysregulated Anger: Whose Anger Is It Anyway?

Overview for Group Leaders

Session 5 continues to be guided by the Middle Circle themes. The exploration of alternative healing, the co-creation of supportive and validating resources, and the balance between honoring the pain of trauma while simultaneously moving forward in life with hope and strength, continues to frame the groupwork in session 5. Additionally, at this juncture of the group process, members should be gaining some level of skill at inducing the relaxation response. As such, new dimensions of relaxation based upon diaphragmatic breathing techniques can be introduced.

Again, the group focus turns more pointedly toward the more specific effects of trauma and early abuse. As noted in earlier sessions, emotional regulation can become problematic for many survivors secondary to the impact of interpersonal violence. **Anger** is one of the more frequently noted unmanageable and dysregulated emotions that can emerge. Individuals may struggle with over-controlled and internalized or under-controlled and externalized (or some variation thereof) expressions of anger as a result of being traumatized and abused. And alcohol, drugs, food, etc., can often serve to grease the wheel and allow these misguided expressions of anger to flow more easily.

The justifiable rage associated with the initial experience of interpersonal violence can become corrupted in its expression as it is filtered through the screen of the Triadic Self. Like a cancer, this distorted and indiscriminate rage seeps into the mind-body-spirit triad and, like an unguided missile, seeks to destroy everything in its path. An important skill in managing anger is to be able to distinguish the justified anger that is a normal part of life from the unresolved anger linked to earlier victimization that is being expressed through the Triadic Self. Gaining clarity regarding what is driving one's anger in a given circumstance allows an individual to *choose* their response rather than operate at the mercy of some indiscriminate and dysregulated source of rage. Choosing and awareness of choice can transform one from being a victim to being an active agent of one's own desires in a very powerful way.

Additionally, in any effort to tame the bucking bronco of anger, it is important to gain a sense of how anger is experienced (i.e., how participants talk, think, feel about, and imagine) anger on multiple levels. It is also essential to understand the direction of anger and to begin to take steps toward pointing it toward the appropriate and deserving target(s).

Finally, because the anger survivors feel is often not their own, they can frequently experience anger as toxic, dangerous, and deadly. Appropriate anger, however, can mobilize and empower people to act in their own best interests. Participants will be given an opportunity to experience the positive healing aspect of healthy anger. Anger, then, becomes recruited into the process of healing; promoting acts of self-care and strength diminishes its power to motivate self-destructive behavior and block the group members' efforts to return to emotional balance.

Group Leaders' Tasks for Session 5

- Guided Relaxation Exercise and Check-In: facilitate relaxation exercise and brief well-being check-in and a go-round of reflections, insights, or actions that emerged in response to last week's session.
- Didactic Component: provide information on discriminating healthy anger from toxic anger and facilitate understanding regarding the direction and expression of anger.
- Process Component: guide the exploration of participants' individual experience (thoughts, feelings, ideas, direction, expression, etc.) of anger and how it gets expressed through the Triadic Self.
- Experiential Component: introduction to Deep Muscle Relaxation (DMR).
- Maintenance: practical guidelines for anger management.

Group Leaders' Pre-Group Preparation for Session 5

1. Review the steps of Deep Muscle Relaxation so that you may facilitate the exercise with ease.
2. Consider tape recording the exercise and providing participants with copies for their use at home.

Group Member Tasks for Session 5

- discriminate between healthy and toxic expressions of anger
- gain insight into their own understanding, expression, and direction of anger as it reveals itself through patterns driven by the Triadic Self
- become familiar with Muscle Relaxation techniques

■Guided Relaxation Exercise and Check-In

Begin with the guided relaxation exercise for 5 minutes. Then use the following questions to guide the go-rounds:

→ Rate your emotional well-being for the past week on a scale from 1–10 and share with the group any actions you took to raise it when it was low. Were you able to *name, feel, and let go?*

(*Probes for Facilitators:
→ Did you have any further insights or reflections related to last week's topic?
→ What, if anything, did you do differently as a result of last week's session?)

HELPFUL HINT
You may want to briefly emphasize that participants should be continuing with their relaxation practice.

■Process Component

Use the following questions as guidelines for the process discussion. You might want to write responses to the opening and closing *brainstorm questions* on the board.

1. Describe how your anger feels to you on the inside.
2. What does your anger look like? (i.e., like the Tazmanian devil, like a dark pool, like a big mountain, etc.)
3. How has your addiction helped regulate dysregulated anger?

GROUP BRAINSTORM QUESTION #1
What words, thoughts, feelings, or images pop into your mind when I say "anger"?

GROUP BRAINSTORM QUESTION #2
Healthy anger can help in the healing process. It can mobilize people to take action in their best interest. It can help make people strong and resilient and give them courage. In what ways has anger helped your healing process, and what expressions and forms has your healthy, nontoxic anger taken?

■Didactic Component

Whose Anger Is It Anyway?

One of the main problems in managing dysregulated anger for survivors of trauma and abuse is being able to make the distinction between justifiable and appropriate anger that is their own versus toxic, destructive anger that belongs to the Triadic Self and is expressed in the form of Trauma Reenactment. The following presentation should help participants to begin to make these distinctions and thus empower them to choose their response instead of being unconsciously driven to respond.

HELPFUL HINTS

It is important to validate and not minimize the participant's experience of rage toward the abuse and their abuser. It is their own, it is appropriate, and it is pointed in the right direction. The central point that you are trying to emphasize is the distinction between appropriate anger and *dysregulated anger*. The dysregulated expression of anger—unconscious, out of control, out of proportion and misdirected—can keep survivors controlled by and at the mercy of their abuser.

Introduction

"We are going to spend some time today talking specifically about anger as a significant emotion that can become dysregulated and toxic when secondary to trauma. There are three dimensions of anger that we will discuss. The first involves distinguishing healthy anger from toxic anger by recognizing the role Trauma Reenactment plays in dysregulated rage; the second and third involve understanding the direction or misdirection (who the anger gets pointed at) and control or dyscontrol (how someone over- or under-manages their anger). While toxic anger (or anger motivated by Trauma Reenactment) can be overwhelming, the session today will help us discover there are ways to manage or eliminate toxic rage and ways to develop healthy anger as a source of power, strength, and resilience."

Dimension #1: Toxic Anger from Trauma Reenactment

Read aloud or paraphrase the following.

Have you ever had the experience of being with another person, either alone or in a group, and having that person look right through you as if you are not there? You know what I mean—someone who knows you are there but they just seem to look through you as if you are invisible, not seeing you at all, almost as though in some weird way and for some unknown reason they are discounting your very existence. You may even speak directly to them, but they don't acknowledge you at all. How does that experience leave you feeling? Angry? Enraged? Ashamed? Worthless?

Most people would blow this kind of encounter off and think little of it. For folks who have suffered abuse and trauma, however, a situation like this can trigger an amplified and intense reaction that may lead to destructive internalized or externalized expressions of rage. What is really happening may in fact be a manifestation of Trauma Reenactment. If we looked at this example from that perspective, who are you really responding to? Maybe not the real individual before you, who could be distracted for any number of reasons unrelated to you, but the Nonprotecting Bystander who refused to see you when you needed most to be seen. This person refused to see what was happening, discounted your signals for help, and turned their back on you as if you were not here . . . as if you were invisible.

Use the illustrations below and on the handout and the following guidelines to further illustrate the idea that *the anger you feel may not be your own*. Be sure to emphasize that making the distinction between healthy and toxic anger is an important step in the process of beginning to manage unmanageable rage.

The anger you feel may not be your own!

Remember this?	What we are talking about now!
Trauma Reenactment	Emotional Reenactment

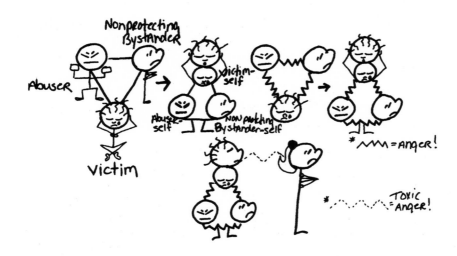

Specifically:
Toxic Anger

Guiding Points

- Briefly review the basics of Trauma Reenactment and the idea of emotional reenactment.
- Underscore the idea that the emotions linked to the past initial trauma (like anger) can get triggered in the present.
- As a result, your emotions (like anger) may actually be expressions of the Triadic Self.

Dimensions 2 and 3: Direction and Control of Anger

Again use the following illustrations (included in the participant's handout) and guidelines to help explain and underscore the point that dysregulated anger may involve rage directed in the wrong direction as well as too much, too little, or too unpredictable a control of anger! Note to the participants that these examples may fit each of them in different situations or different life stages.

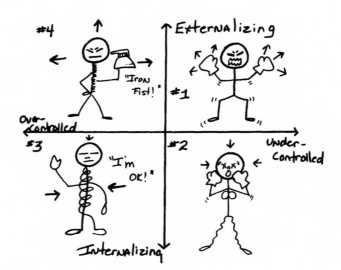

Guiding Points

Direction and control of anger can be seen on a dimensional continuum with extreme or variable expressions along any radius indicating dysregulation.

- Direction: anger can be seen as pointed outward at others (*externalized*) or inward at the self (*internalized*).
- Control: the expression of anger can be seen as out-of-control (*under*-controlled) or too controlled (*over*-controlled).

- The four extreme or dysregulated expressions of anger as demonstrated by the dimensional continuum:
    - externalized and under-controlled=acts out against others, short fuse, "hair trigger" temper
    - under-controlled and internalizing=impulsive, directs rage inward, self-harming
    - internalizing and over-controlled="tightly wound," appears in control, anger directed inward, depressed, may have physical problems
    - over-controlled and externalizing="control freak," rages against others but in a focused calculated way, "rules with an iron fist" attitude
- Of course, many survivors fluctuate wildly along these dimensions of direction and control as a result of emotional dysregulation.

Use the following to draw the didactic presentation to a conclusion. How do you distinguish healthy anger from *toxic anger*?

Healthy Anger	Toxic Anger
You can own it.	It belongs to the Triadic Self.
It is an appropriate "fit" for the situation.	It is extreme and out of proportion.
It is pointed in the right direction.	It is pointed in the wrong direction.

Ask participants to identify other ways they can distinguish healthy anger from toxic anger.

■Experiential Component

Deep Muscle Relaxation

The following is an introduction to Deep Muscle Relaxation. Participants may add this to their regular relaxation practice or use it to help with sleep difficulty. The nature of this exercise—contracting and releasing muscle groupings—provides a positive metaphor for anger management and can be used during the exercise. For example, when the muscle is contracting, participants can imagine the tension of their anger. When they release the contraction, participants can imagine releasing and letting go of their anger.

Step 1. Explain to participants that you will guide them through an exercise called Deep Muscle Relaxation. The exercise involves alternating between tensing and relaxing different muscle groups so that participants can make better

HELPFUL HINTS

You may want to make a tape recording and provide it for those participants who feel they will not be able to remember the exercise. This will allow them to do the exercise at home on their own more easily.

Be sure to inform individuals with pain or injuries to use their best judgment and either skip over any uncomfortable areas during the exercise or to try it gently and stop if they experience any discomfort or pain.

Facilitators need to direct participants to hold the tension for five seconds and to observe (or notice, focus on, study . . .) the release for 15–20 seconds.

distinctions between feelings of tension and feelings of relaxation. Note to participants that they may or may not feel effects initially but that practice will help.

Step 2. Ask participants to make a mental note of their current level of tension on a scale of 1–10.

Step 3. Invite participants to get comfortable in their chairs, with their feet flat on the floor, and arms and hands uncrossed and resting in their laps or on the arms of the chair. Direct them to close their eyes or to allow their gaze to fall in a soft focus on the floor a foot or two ahead of them.

Step 4. Direct participants to turn their focus inward and begin the relaxation response. Guide participants in this endeavor for a minute or so and then introduce the exercise.

Step 5. "*Continue your deep breathing as I speak to you and give you the following information. This exercise is designed to help you learn how to relax your body even more deeply. I will be guiding you through the entire exercise. In just a few minutes I will ask you to contract or tense different muscle groupings in your body. You will contract and hold the contraction for a count of five. At that point, you will release the contraction. As you do so, I want you to focus your attention on the* sensation *of releasing the tension. You will focus on and study these sensations for 15–20 seconds. What does it feel like? Does it feel warm? Tingly? Heavy? Tune in and be aware of what it feels like in your body to release the contraction, and enjoy the contrast between the tensed state and the relaxed state. We will start with the hands and arms, then move into the head and face, then back down into the neck and shoulders, the torso and back, hips, legs, and down through the feet. If at any time you feel discomfort or pain, stop the exercise and either return to your diaphragmatic breathing or try again at your own discretion.*"

Step 6. "*Let's begin. I want you now to turn your attention to your hands and arms. Put all your focus into your hands and arms even as you continue to breathe deep and slow. When I tell you to contract, I want you to pull your hands into very tight fists and flex the muscles in your forearm and upper arm bending your arms at the elbow, squeezing the muscles and holding for a count of five. When I say to release, I want you to release your fists and arms and allow them to relax. Okay . . . contract and hold—1 . . . squeeze those fists tight and make those biceps bulge—2 . . . and hold—3 . . . holding tight—4 . . . still holding—5 . . . and release . . . relax . . . let go . . . . Allow your hands and arms to completely release the tension they are holding. . . . Notice how they feel as you relax them. . . . Do they feel warm, heavy, light? What is the sensation in your hands and arms as you feel them relax? . . Just notice and be aware. . . . Notice the contrast between the feeling of tension and the feeling of relaxation. . . . Allow yourself to let go and relax even more."* (The relaxation phase should last between 15–20 seconds each time.)

Step 7. The exercise continues in this manner as participants are guided through the progressive relaxation technique. It is important that the leader of the exercise do the following each time:

- Identify the next muscle grouping you are moving to.
- Provide participants with instructions on *how* to contract that muscle group.
- Give them the cue to *contract* and hold for the count of five.
- Give them the cue to *release*.
- Guide them to focus on the *sensation* of release and relaxation following each contraction; direct them to study, observe, and focus on the contrast or distinction between those sensations for 15–20 seconds following the release cue.
- Scan and monitor the group to make sure everyone understands the directions.

Step 8. After completing the hands and arms, bypass the neck and shoulders for the moment. Direct participants to contract their face muscles by squeezing their eyes, nose, and mouth together towards the center of their face.

Step 9. Next, move to the jaw and neck. Instruct participants to pull the corners of their mouths back toward their ears and to tighten the neck muscles. When they release this contraction, make sure they release any tension in the jaw and instruct them to allow their jaw to fall slack and to hang open.

Step 10. Move to the shoulders. To contract the muscles, direct participants to raise their shoulders in a shrug upward to their earlobes while at the same time pulling their chin to their chest.

Step 11. Next, have participants tighten the muscles in their torso (stomach and chest). Instruct them to tighten up as if they are about to prepare for a blow to the stomach.

Step 12. Have participants move their focus to their lower back and hips. Instruct them to contract these muscles by squeezing the buttocks together tightly.

Step 13. Now have participants shift their focus into their legs. Direct them to stretch both legs forward, squeeze their legs together, and point their toes toward the ceiling.

Step 14. Finally, have participants contract the muscles in their feet by tightly curling their toes under and flexing their feet upward.

Step 15. Allow participants some time to sit with the experience of relaxation in their bodies. Encourage them to tune into any remaining tension in their body and to contract, count to five, and release on their own.

Step 16. To conclude, direct participants to bring their focus back into the room. Ask them to return their focus to the room at their own pace when they are ready, then ask them to open their eyes or turn their gaze back upward to eye level. Spend a few minutes processing this exercise with the group. Ask participants to rate their level of tension once again on a scale from 1–10 and see if there are any changes. Address any concerns, questions, problem spots, or confusion, and encourage them to try this at home in addition to the relaxation response.

■ Maintenance

Stopping the Locomotion!

Whatever the form of your dysregulated anger, do the following to try and manage it in the moment!

1. Stop *before you act.*
2. Name *the feeling before you react.*
3. Think *before you speak.*
4. Release *the tension before you choose.*

In order to better manage your anger, the very first thing you have to do is slow things down! Once you do, you have a better chance of choosing your own course of action rather than being driven by toxic rage! Practice releasing tension before you act or speak!

Cultivating Courage: Moving beyond Anxiety and Fear

Overview for Group Leaders

Session 6 marks the halfway point of the 12-week intervention process. In this session, Middle Circle themes of establishing healing alternatives, letting in support, and exploring issues of both pain and hope, continue to provide structure for the group process. Additionally, however, the careful transition to the Inner Circle (which centers on witnessing individual histories, validating new stories, and cultivating connections) begins as the very roots of interpersonal violence are brought into the light.

Anxiety—the focus of this session—can be a debilitating and paralyzing experience for trauma survivors. Intense levels of fear and anxiety can cause the clinical phenomenon of **dissociation** to occur. At the time of the initial trauma, dissociation serves an adaptive role by helping the individual continue to function in the face of an overwhelming threat to their personal integrity. As the traumatic stressor continues unmodified and escalates, individuals move through increasing levels of dissociation. Primary dissociation occurs when cognition or thoughts are split off and separated from one's experience in the face of a threat. Secondary dissociation occurs when emotions or affect fail to be experienced during overwhelming stress. And tertiary dissociation occurs when the stressor is so overwhelming that an individual's consciousness splits and a separate "self" develops in order to deal with the trauma. When an individual is chronically triggered, this initially adaptive pattern of response becomes the *only* pattern of response available in the face of fear and stress.

Secondary to the disruption of the arousal system, trauma and abuse can also leave one prone to **hyperarousal** (an easily and frequently engaged fight or flight response), **hypervigilance** (an inability to lower one's guard), or an increased **startle response** (a hair-trigger response to innocuous cues). When a survivor has flashbacks, memories, or some benign reminder of the initial trauma, the body can respond *as if the trauma is happening all over again in the present!* As a result, a pervasive sense of fear and anxiety colors one's life and can lead to disturbances of daily functioning such as sleep difficulties, a lack of attention or concentration, etc.

One researcher has said that the failure to process the dissociated memory of the traumatic event is the essence of trauma. It is the essence of Trauma Reenactment as well. It is the fragmented and unintegrated memory of the initial experience that drives reenactment behavior. This leads to pervasive, unmanageable fear, chaos, and isolation in the mind-body-spirit of a survivor. It becomes, critical, therefore, to address this dimension of Trauma Reenactment. The goal of this chapter is to guide participants to identify this cycle and develop new ways to respond to old threats. The ghosts of trauma need to be released as survivors return to the land of the living and find new ways of being, and of being safe, in the world.

Group Leaders' Tasks for Session 6

Group leaders should facilitate the following group processes:

- Guided Relaxation Exercise and Check-In: facilitate relaxation exercise, lead group in well-being check-in and discussion of gains or changes made over the past week secondary to the information and process provided thus far.
- Didactic Component: information provided on anxiety and fear associated with trauma and abuse as manifested in dissociative phenomena, hyperarousal, hypervigilance, etc.
- Process Component: facilitate exploration of issues that have emerged in participants' lives because of the fear they continue to carry with them as a result of the trauma.
- Experiential Component: lead group in grounding visualization exercise designed to provide participants with a safe grounding alternative to managing fear and anxiety by their addiction or other self-harming phenomena.
- Maintenance: cultivating courage in the face of fear.

Group Leaders' Pre-Group Preparation for Session 6

1. Review the information clusters thoroughly so you can easily present the material.
2. Bring a variety of grounding objects (rocks, flowers, leaves, textured fabric) for participants to choose from during the experiential exercise.

Group Member Goals for Session 6

Group members should achieve the following goals:

- gain a basic understanding of the role of fear and anxiety in trauma and abuse
- acquire a basic working knowledge of the three levels of dissociation and the relationship to trauma and abuse
- articulate their own experience of fear and anxiety related to trauma
- gain insight into the role that addictions and self-harming play in their efforts to manage unmanageable fear and anxiety
- learn a grounding visualization exercise as an alternative to other self-harming forms of soothing and centering

■Guided Relaxation Exercise and Check-In

Following the opening relaxation exercise (six minutes in duration) group leaders should facilitate a well-being check-in for participants and encourage reflection on any progress made over the week. Use the following questions to guide the brief check-in.

→ On a scale from 1–10, how would you rate your overall emotional well-being this week?

Prompts (for facilitators' use in further exploring check-in issues):
→ If it was low, what steps did you take to feel better?
→ If it was high, what steps did you take to get there?

■Didactic Component

Invite group members to respond to the following "poll." Be sure that you allow them to not respond publicly if they do not feel comfortable doing so.

HELPFUL HINT

Some of the information in this section is based upon earlier presentations on traumatic stress and the fight or flight response. Feel free to refer to earlier discussions and presentations and to use any helpful handouts from earlier sessions.

Group Poll

How many of you have ever experienced the following phenomena:

___ "spacing out"	___ loss of time
___ out-of-body experience	___ poor memory
___ difficulty concentrating	___ daydreaming
___ difficulty sleeping	___ feeling "unreal"
___ feeling like you are in a dream	___ confusion
___ altered perception of pain	___ flashbacks
___ altered perception of body	___ tunnel vision
___ fragmented memories	___ nightmares
___ emotional numbing	___ feeling easily startled
___ separate inner "self"	___ hypervigilance
___ chronic feelings of dread	___ panic attacks

How Come I'm Still Afraid?

Use the following vignettes on disordered arousal and dissociation to begin the presentation on how trauma and abuse contribute to chronic anxiety and fear.

Vignette #1: (illustrates disordered arousal such as hypervigilance, panic, exaggerated startle response, chronic feelings of being unsafe, etc.)

Kelly has trouble being in situations where she is in close contact with others. She lives in fear, trapped by her frequent panic attacks and her chronic feelings of being unsafe. Loud sounds cause her to react with an exaggerated startle response: she jumps, gasps loudly, or sometimes screams. She can't go any-where—even when she is in a familiar, safe neighborhood—without constantly looking over her shoulder to make sure she can't see anyone in her vicinity.

Vignette #2: (illustrates dissociation: going numb, dazing out, etc.)

Ronnie says that often she doesn't realize that blocks of time have passed, time that she has no memory about. She also notices that others tell her she seems to be noticeably "somewhere else" during conversations and activities; she experiences herself as not being present (or "spaced out") whenever situations make her nervous or angry. She also experiences her mind and body becoming "numb" for long periods of time as if she is frozen or disembodied.

Use the following **information clusters** and the handouts on pp. 191–193 to guide the didactic presentation on fear and anxiety. Use your own discretion regarding the depth at which you want to present the material in the information clusters. Base your decision on group interest and need. Be sure to make appropriate links to the earlier group poll.

Information Cluster #1

Brief Review

"You now have a lot of information about what happens during trauma and abuse. You have learned about the fight or flight response and how it triggers mental, as well as body-based, reactions that are designed to help us protect ourselves when we are threatened. You also learned that sometimes this initially adaptive response can cause a lot of problems when an individual is unable to return to balance or homeostasis following the initial trauma. The way the initial event gets processed in the body, the mind, and through the spirit can cause a lot of difficulty later on. As a result, 3-D distress, or difficulty along multiple dimensions, can occur and can often lead to Trauma Reenactment."

Ask the group if they have any questions regarding any of this information. Clarify any misunderstandings before moving on to the next information cluster.

Information Cluster #2

Continuum of Fear

"During a traumatic experience, one's anxiety level will continue to increase as the perceived threat persists and nothing happens to change it. Autonomic arousal, or the fight or flight response, gets triggered because of the trauma, and it continues to escalate as the risk of harm continues unabated. Anxiety changes to hyperarousal and can escalate to stark fear very quickly, moving rapidly up the continuum of fear as the intensity of the trauma increases. In addition to the experiences already identified regarding the fight or flight response, many people experience alterations in consciousness at the time of traumatic stress. The more intense the stressor or threat, the more acutely someone may experience these altered states of consciousness. This is another clue to understanding why the traumatic memory may not become fully integrated into consciousness."

Information Cluster #3

Altered Arousal

"Just like our discussion of emotion dysregulation, a victim of trauma or abuse may have experienced damage to their arousal 'thermostat.' As a result, individuals may struggle with disruptions in their ability to modulate their anxious arousal and may be more easily triggered to respond to memories, flashbacks, or innocuous triggers with a full-blown fight or flight response (or something similar to it). Some of these experiences include:

- *Hyperarousal, an easily triggered fight or flight reaction*
- *Hypervigilance, a guarded watchfulness due to chronic unsafe feelings can contribute disruption in sleep cycle*
- *Exaggerated Startle Response, when someone is easily startled and responds out of proportion to the stimulus or trigger*
- *Panic Attacks, which are intense feelings of dread along with increased physiological symptoms like heart palpitations, shortness of breath, shakiness, sweating, tunnel vision, etc."*

Information Cluster #4

Altered Consciousness

Paraphrase the following information:

Altered states of consciousness may occur as hyperarousal increases. These alterations in consciousness or dissociative phenomena are initially adaptive and occur during the initial trauma to help people continue to function in spite of the threat. However, as the threat continues, there can be a progression from extreme arousal to dissociation.

Dissociation of the Mind. Primary dissociation is the first level of dissociation and entails a splitting off of cognition from consciousness in the face of extreme threat. This is reflected in individual experience as over- or under-integration of the traumatic event. This type of recall can lead to intrusive recollections, flashbacks, and nightmares and can lead to PTSD.

Dissociation of the Body. Secondary dissociation involves the splitting off of affect or emotion from consciousness in the face of an extreme danger or threat to personal integrity. This is also referred to as peritraumatic dissociation and can include out-of-body experiences (i.e., watching the event happen as if from a distance); altered or distorted experiences of time, place, or person; feeling "unreal"; confusion; bewilderment; changes in capacity for pain perception; alterations in body image; and tunnel vision.

Dissociation of the Spirit. Tertiary dissociation is the most extreme form of dissociative phenomenon. It involves a complete split from consciousness and the development of a different ego state to contain the trauma. This can sometimes lead to dissociative disorders.

Some level of dissociation during a stressful and traumatic experience occurs to most people. What happens in the aftermath can become most problematic for survivors of trauma and abuse. For example, hyperarousal secondary to flashbacks can lead a person to dissociate chronically, and it becomes their only response in the face of any misperceived threat. (Again, use your own judgment regarding the details you want to present on dissociative experiences.)

Information Cluster #5

So Why Am I Still Afraid?

"Hyperarousal and dissociation are **adaptive** responses to extreme threat. The problem is that memories of traumatic events may be either over-integrated or under-integrated in memory. As a result, things—people, places, objects, feelings, thoughts, memories, nightmares, flashbacks, etc.—in the present that are reminiscent of the past can trigger levels of fear and anxiety equal to or even greater than that experienced during the initial trauma! The fearful response is generalized to (or linked with) experiences that are not actually threatening. As a result, a person may develop a chronic fear-based pattern of responding to misperceived threats by hyperarousal, which can lead to dissociation. This sets up a cycle of trigger → arousal → dissociation that is at the heart of Trauma Reenactment. In this case, the initial fear and anxiety of the trauma gets reenacted repeatedly and becomes a 'hard-wired' part of the response system.

"The past stays alive in the present in many subtle and not-so-subtle ways for survivors of trauma and abuse. That is why fear and anxiety may continue to disrupt one's life long after the trauma is over. That is also why many individuals choose alcohol, drugs, or other addictions to try and manage the unmanageable fear and anxiety. Now, it is time for you to put the ghosts of trauma to rest . . . to move beyond Trauma Reenactment as a way of being in the world . . . to recognize and embrace the courage that you carry within—the courage that has helped you survive!"

Allow time and space for the group to ask questions and gain clarity of these issues of hyperarousal and dissociation before moving to the Process Component.

■Process Component

Use the following questions to guide the process discussion on anxiety and fear.

1. What are you now most afraid of or anxious about?

2. How have you used your addiction to calm your fears and reduce your anxiety?

3. How might you now deal with these fears and worries differently?

■ Experiential Component

The relaxation response has already been introduced to help manage hyper-arousal. Deep Muscle Relaxation is also very effective with anxiety. The following exercise is designed to guide participants in grounding themselves in a safe place when they are feeling anxious or frightened and can be used as a conscious alternative to dissociation.

HELPFUL HINTS

Use soothing music with this relaxation exercise.

Allow participants to choose between closing their eyes and externally focusing on an object.

Inform participants of the nature of the exercise before beginning.

Be sure to have items for participants to choose from to hold during the exercise such as rocks, flowers, leaves, textured fabric, etc. You might suggest that they choose an item that reflects the safe haven they will create in their imaginations.

Safe Haven Exercise

Step 1. Have participants engage in the relaxation response.

Step 2. Have participants pick a place that they imagine makes them feel safe and unafraid. This can be a room in their house, a sandy beach, a deep, shady forest, a favorite chair—wherever they might feel safe and unafraid.

Step 3. Now invite them to imagine this scene as vividly as possible, to create it in specific detail in their imaginations. Ask them to imagine the colors, textures, smells, sounds, sensations, etc., that are present in the setting. Guide their efforts in painting the scene vividly by suggesting different possibilities (i.e., Are there animals in your scene? What are they doing? Is there a breeze? What are the things you smell in your safe place?).

Step 4. Once the scene has been created, invite participants to enter the scene, to imagine what they are doing, feeling, and thinking as they move about or stay still in this safe place. Again offer neutral cues to guide the participants' efforts (i.e., Is the sun shining? Can you feel it against your skin? Is it warm or cool outside? Can you feel the earth against your body?).

Step 5. Allow participants to remain in their scene in silence for several minutes before inviting them to return to the room at their own pace.

Step 6. Spend a few minutes processing the experience with the group. For those who had difficulty, remind them that the exercise may take practice, but that over time this can be a very effective relaxation method. Inform the group members that they can go to this safe place anytime they choose. It is the choosing that makes this a powerful experience.

■Maintenance

Cultivating Courage Day by Day

Invite participants to reflect on the theme of *courage* in their own lives. How do they define courage? How are they courageous every day? Have them keep in mind that real courage often happens in quiet moments with no fanfare; sometimes it's in the simple decision to take one step and one day at a time. Encourage each participant to see themselves as the hero in their own lives as they work hard and take actions to save their own lives. Invite them to make a list of the large and small acts of courage they engage in daily. Have them post the list in their homes to remind themselves of their own "brave hearts"!

The Body Remembers What the Spirit Seeks to Forget

Overview for Group Leaders

In session 7 the group process moves into a deeper exploration of the Inner Circle themes. Participants may reveal parts of their personal histories in more detail as they relate to session topics. It is important that each shared story, and its storyteller, be acknowledged, validated, and emotionally held by the group. In so doing, feelings of isolation can dissolve, a connection to others can deepen, and new stories of healing, strength, and resilience can emerge.

The primary focus of this session is for group members to understand how their experience of trauma has—both literally and metaphorically—become lodged in their bodies.

Research has shown that more than 80 percent of people who struggle with a wide array of serious but vague illnesses have histories of childhood abuse or trauma. Such disorders as fibromyalgia, irritable bowel syndrome, chronic fatigue syndrome, unexplained pelvic and GI pain, and chronic back pain, may originate with trauma. As such, it is an important factor in the amelioration of 3-D distress to recognize and address the possible physical manifestations of trauma in the body.

While the exact mechanisms by which trauma translates into physical illnesses remain unclear, there are new areas of understanding that can serve to enlighten our current knowledge and promote healing and empowerment among survivors. For example, the mind, including the memory, is actually located *throughout our entire body!* This helps make sense of how frequently, and often intensely, trauma survivors experience heightened physiological arousal or emotional dysregulation by a simple innocuous touch, smell, or bodily sensation.

Thus **bodily reenactment** is a response to current bodily experiences that are reminiscent of initial trauma.

You may recall from earlier sessions how unprocessed trauma material or aspects of the trauma that may have not been fully processed and integrated by the higher order brain functions. Some theorists believe that this "undigested" material becomes lodged in the memory of the body and could be the source of many unexplained illnesses; this theory would explain why so many survivors of trauma and abuse battle a myriad of puzzling physical complaints of vague or ill-defined origins.

Exploring the often invalidating response to their physical pain by the medical community, family, or friends can help affirm participants' difficult struggle with this complex issue. Additionally, supporting their efforts to name their experience and provide new tools for "digesting" the "undigested" can serve to cultivate an effective alternative to this deceptive body-based response to trauma. Participants can begin to let go of the pain they carry within their bodies as they take action to first recognize the discomforting load they have held for so long, share it with others, and then release it.

Group Leaders' Tasks for Session 7

Group leaders should facilitate the following group processes:

- Guided Relaxation Exercise and Check-In: guide relaxation exercise and lead group well-being check-in; ask about insights, questions, or changes initiated in response to last week's session; lead the group in the body scan exercise.
- Didactic Component: provide information on how trauma is held in the body and can emerge in the form of physical pain, discomfort, or illness.
- Process Component: guide participants in the examination of dominant narratives related to their efforts to address their physical pain; also explore with each participant where they may carry the pain of their trauma in their bodies.
- Experiential Component: guide participants through an expressive arts exercise designed to help them identify and transform the experience of pain in their bodies.
- Maintenance: introduce journaling as a mechanism to help heal the body and guide one to improved health and quality of life.

Group Leaders' Pre-Group Preparation for Session 7

1. Prepare paper figures for Experiential Component in advance (see pages 112 and 113 for further details).

2. Review the pathway of somatization before presenting it to the group.

Group Member Tasks for Session 7

Group members should achieve the following goals:

- initiate a body scan as part of their relaxation practice
- gain an understanding of how trauma can become lodged in the body and translated as physical discomfort and illness
- gain insight into the dominant messages they received regarding their physical complaints and identify where they experience trauma in their own bodies
- actively explore and reframe their experience of physical pain secondary to trauma

■Guided Relaxation Exercise and Check-In

Following a brief go-round of an emotional and physical well-being check-in, invite the participants to engage in the relaxation response process. You may want to use music for this expanded relaxation exercise. When everyone settles into their diaphragmatic breathing pattern, read the following paragraphs aloud.

Step 1. *"Continue to breathe deeply in and deeply out. As you do so, I want you to imagine a glowing ball of warmth and light at the center of your chest."*

Step 2. *"Imagine that the glowing ball at the center of your chest brings light, warmth, energy, and healing as it radiates outward."*

Step 3. *"I want you to now place the glowing orb at the top of your head and slowly allow it to move downward through your body. As it moves, let yourself feel the warmth and healing energy of its light as it moves through your body."*

Step 4. *"When you come across an area of your body that is tense or painful, allow the glowing orb to pause there. Take several deep and cleansing breaths, breathing through the tension. . . . Allow your breath to move through and dispel the tension or discomfort you are holding and let the warmth of the golden ball of light flood the area with healing energy and light."*

Step 5. *"Allow the orb to move gently throughout your body, pausing as needed and then moving on. Feel its radiating warmth and energy, and feel your body releasing tension through your breath."*

Step 6. *"When the golden ball of light has moved all through your body, allow yourself a moment or two to sit in this relaxed state and then gently bring your focus back to the room. Move at your own pace and, when you are ready, open your eyes or return your gaze to eye level."*

Allow participants a few moments to comment on this exercise. At the conclusion, you should be able to segue smoothly into today's topic on how the body carries the memory and pain of trauma and abuse.

■ Didactic Component

The Body Remembers What the Spirit Seeks to Forget

Open the didactic portion of today's group by reading aloud the following vignette.

> Jan experiences chronic headaches and abdominal pain considered to have no clear organic basis by medical providers who have examined her. She, like other women imprisoned by TR, is often mistreated and invalidated by professionals who think she should be able to overcome her pain. Reflective of her early experience of abuse, her pain is minimized and her needs devalued. Once again she finds no protection, no safety, and no healing from those who are supposed to care for her.

"How might we understand this woman's experience? How does trauma to the body translate into pain and illness in the body? In order to discuss this, we need to revisit some material that was introduced earlier. First, let's take a quick true/false quiz about information on the body, memory, and physical illness."

True/False Quiz

1. Memory is located in the brain.
   (This is **false**. *Memory cells found in the brain are found throughout the entire body! Even in your little toe!*)
2. During traumatic experiences, the part of the brain associated with speech and language decreases in activity while the part of the brain that is associated with emotion increases in activity.
   (This is **true**, *which is why many traumatic events have often been referred to as experiences of "speechless terror."*)
3. During trauma, memory may become "hard-wired" (or imprinted strongly) in your memory.
   (This is **true**, *but traumatic memories can also be under-consolidated, or imprinted in partial, incomplete, or weak ways.*)
4. Suppressing negative emotions can lead to impaired immune system functioning and illnesses.

(This is **true**. *Research indicates that expressing and processing negative experiences and events can improve your immune system functioning and overall health.*)

5. Your pain and illness is all in your head.
   (This is **false!**)

6. The mind-body connection is a highly complex and interrelated relationship—what affects the mind also affects the body.
   (This is **true!**)

7. Your pain and illness are **real**!
   (This is **true!**)

HELPFUL HINTS

Be sure to use the handout to help guide this discussion.

Be sure to emphasize that the following discussion is an oversimplification of a very complex and not yet clearly understood process.

Do You Remember . . .

Overwhelming trauma triggers the fight or flight response.

↓

Perceptions of the trauma then take a shortcut, bypassing the part of the brain that evaluates, processes, labels, categorizes, and integrates perceptions and experiences into memory in a way that makes sense.

↓

Because this process gets bypassed, emotions linked with overwhelming, traumatic experiences may not be fully processed.

↓

New Information . . .
As a result, unprocessed, unnamed emotions can be experienced as physical sensations in the body. (sort of like "unidentifiable body emotions")

↓

These **body emotions** can get activated by memories of the initial trauma, stress, or fatigue; the onset of emotions is similar to those experienced during the initial trauma.(sort of like "body reenactment")

Chronic activation of these nameless emotions in the body can potentially lead to physical discomfort, a disruption of systemic functioning, and illnesses in the body

Allow some time for questions, answers, and insights from the group.

■Process Component

Use the following questions as guidelines for the process discussion.

1. What have been the dominant messages or most common responses and reactions that you have received from others when you have been sick or in physical pain? (i.e., "It's all in your head," "You are making yourself sick," "You are a hypochondriac," "You are being a drama queen").
2. What reactions or responses would have been more helpful to you?
3. Where do you think you carry the pain of your trauma experience in your body?
4. Are there ways in which your addiction helped you to manage unmanageable physical difficulties?
5. Are there ways in which you think your experience of trauma has made your body stronger and more resilient?

■Experiential Component

This exercise should help participants to identify the remnants of traumatic pain in their bodies and begin the process of transforming their relationship to, and experience of, their pain.

Sample:

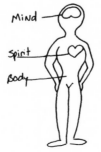  

HELPFUL HINTS

Leaders should prepare paper doll figures ahead of time (about 15 inches tall).

Be sure to have a variety of art supplies including markers, crayons, colored paper, etc.

You could play a soothing piece of music during this exercise.

Allow enough time for the group to complete this exercise and share their final creation with the group.

Step 1. Pass out the paper doll figures to the group members and offer the following instructions:

"This is a two-part exercise. For the first half of the exercise, please show us where your pain is—what it looks and feels like—in your body by writing or drawing images on one side of the figure. You can draw a picture, write words, poetry, or a story—whatever you need to do to express how it feels in your body. You may have a number of different painful experiences. That is okay. Draw or write about as many as you can. Use the whole side of the figure if you want. This is about your experience and expression of the pain you carry inside."

Step 2. When participants have completed one side of the figure, offer the following instructions:

"Now, flip your figure over. I want you to draw or write positive, healing images, words, stories, etc., in the same areas where you indicated you held your pain. Be sure to create a positive, healing 'response' image for every painful one on the other side."

Step 3. When everyone finishes, allow members to share their creations with each other. Ask them to bring the figures home and place them in a conspicuous area with the positive side visible!

■ Maintenance

Journaling—A Gift to Your Spirit

Writing about negative experiences helps improve health and well-being. If participants have not yet begun a journal, encourage them to do so. Journaling has many positive benefits in the healing process. At the close of the session briefly brainstorm and review these positive benefits with the group. Emphasize that journaling is an important factor in maintaining change and in monitoring the ongoing healing process in one's life.

Your Body Is a Gift

Overview for Group Leaders

Session 8 moves the group deeper into the Inner Circle. Connections deepen and isolation dissolves as pieces of the trauma puzzle are revealed and start to fall into place. Confusing and chaotic patterns of behavior come into focus and begin to make sense in the context of Trauma Reenactment. As participants increasingly share their own experiences and bear witness to others, more room for new images and identities other than the "trauma survivor" can emerge.

We all have ideas about our bodies and we imagine how we do or do not look like to others. Some of these ideas may be accurate; others are distorted. Our culture forces us to draw conclusions about our bodies based upon popular standards. Therefore, many women struggle with negative body images and unrealistic ideals that fail to match up with the "norms" often dictated by Hollywood, the media, and advertising. This struggle seems universal, expected, and, irritatingly, acceptable. It is an ongoing struggle as social tides shift and people race to respond to the most current trend.

However, this same struggle for survivors of trauma and abuse is frequently a battle to destruction, if not death. Childhood abuse and trauma can further distort the lens through which first the child, then the adult, views their body. Not only are they seeing themselves through the critical social lens we all live with, but they have the added burden of seeing themselves through the twisted lens of the Triadic Self—that is, through the eyes of the Abuser, the Victim, and the Nonprotecting Bystander.

In the aftermath of trauma and abuse, many survivors feel that their bodies have betrayed them. Others wish they could shed their bodies like a snake sheds its skin. Some poison their bodies with alcohol and drugs, while others seek to destroy themselves by starving or wounding themselves. Still others hide their bodies from view or "pad" themselves with extra weight for protection. Early in the healing process, few survivors have the capacity to value their body for the extraordinary mechanism that it really is. Instead, they seek to destroy what their abuser could not.

This session should help participants to begin to transform their negative and self-destructive relationship with their bodies into one in which they honor their body as a vessel for their emerging and healing self. Shifting the lens from the body as a "curse" to the body as a "gift," can guide group members in first seeing, and then acting as, who they really are in their bodies: precious and valued beings of a miraculous variety of shapes and sizes who have amazing capacities for resilience, strength, and healing.

Group Leaders' Tasks for Session 8

Group leaders should facilitate the following group processes:

- Guided Relaxation Exercise and Check-In: facilitate a brief well-being check-in and a go-round on any reflections or thoughts regarding last week's topic on somatization. Most of this group session will be spent on an introductory movement and relaxation exercise designed to help participants tune in to their bodies.
- Didactic Component: information presented on how survivors of trauma and abuse come to view their bodies through the distorted lens of the Triadic Self (i.e., the Abuser, the Victim, and the Nonprotecting Bystander).
- Process Component: examine questions regarding current ideas and images that participants hold about their bodies. The guided discussion opens the way for group members to reconsider views and think about their bodies in new and positive ways.
- Experiential Component: an active and engaging exploration of the image of the body as a "gift."
- Maintenance: taking care of the details—treating your body as if it is something you care about!

Group Leaders' Pre-Group Preparation for Session 8

1. Practice the introductory movement exercise several times before presenting it to the group so that your transitions will be smooth and comfortable.
2. Obtain materials for the experiential exercise in advance—get gift boxes, wrapping paper, construction paper, markers, and blank cards.

Group Member Goals for Session 8

Group members should achieve the following goals:

- begin to increase their awareness of bodily sensations and experiences
- receive information on how trauma or abuse has impacted their body image
- identify their own body image distortions and examine patterns of abusing, victimizing, or not protecting their bodies
- discover positive reframes or reconceptualizations of their body image
- briefly examine how self-care contributes to transforming a negative body image

■Guided Relaxation Exercise and Check-In

This week's check-in will be an introductory experiential exercise. Inform group members of this small deviation from the usual format. Do give them an opportunity to participate in a brief well-being check-in or to comment on any thoughts, reflections, or insights regarding the last session's topic.

After starting the music, say the following paragraphs aloud.

"Today we are going to talk about our bodies. In later sessions, we will discuss the relationship between trauma or abuse and pain in our bodies. During this session we are going to look at our ideas, images, thoughts, and feelings about and toward our bodies. However, before we begin, we are going to do a brief exercise that is designed to help us tune in to very simple dimensions of our bodies. Because trauma and abuse can interfere with one's ability to attend to feelings and sensations, we want to try to do so slowly and comfortably. We will move very slowly in simple and nonthreatening ways. Be sure you are participating at the level of your own comfort. If you feel any physical discomfort, immediately discontinue the exercise." (pause)

Step 1. *"Everyone should stand with their feet approximately shoulders width apart, arms and hands hanging down at your sides. Close your eyes and follow my voice or allow your gaze to fall forward on the floor 1–2 feet ahead of you. It is not necessary to look at me unless you become uncertain of the directions I am giving you. Just follow my voice."* (pause)

Step 2. *"Allow your focus to turn inward upon the rhythmic cycle of your breath. Let your cares and worries fall away and attend only to the in-and-out pattern of your breath. Notice what moves when you breathe in and what moves when you breathe out. Notice how your body feels as you begin to let your muscles relax. See if you can tune into the partnership between your breath and your body."* (pause)

HELPFUL HINTS

Use a soothing, slow selection of music for the exercise.

Move and speak very slowly in a soothing tone throughout; always articulate what participants should be doing while you actually do it.

Encourage everyone to engage at their own level of comfort.

Pause briefly (5–10 seconds) between each step.

Monitor the group and do not move on to the next step until you are clear that everyone has understood the instruction.

Although the instructions appear lengthy, this exercise should not take more than 10–15 minutes.

Step 3. *"Continue to allow your breath to deepen and slow down—breathe deeply in through your nose and out through your mouth. As you do so, I want you to imagine that there is a warm, glowing sphere at the center of your chest, a ball that radiates light and energy throughout your body as if it were the center of your body's universe. This radiant orb pulsates with positive energy and healing right from the center of your chest, and you can feel the energy spread throughout your body."* (pause)

Step 4. *"Breathe deeply and slowly. . . . Just stand still and be for a moment . . . relax . . . feel the energy from the sphere flow through your body . . . feel the tug of gravity on your body."* (pause)

Step 5. *"Continue to breathe and relax as you listen. Right now, you are standing with your weight on both feet. Your center, or the place where you imagine the golden orb of light, is directly above the middle point between your two feet. Not yet, but when I tell you to shift, I want you to shift most of your weight onto the right foot. The radiating sphere of your center will then be positioned directly above your right foot and leg. Now, very gently, very slowly, shift your weight."* (pause)

Step 6. *"Most of your weight and the sphere should now both be over the right foot. Notice how this feels different from standing on both feet. . . . How does the pull of gravity feel different? Did you stop breathing as you moved? What are your left foot and leg doing right now? How do your right leg and foot feel right now? Just tune in and notice these things for a moment."* (pause)

Step 7. *"Now, continue to breathe and notice the experience of your body as you move your right arm upward until it is reaching for a spot somewhere between where the ceiling ends and the walls start. The radiating sphere is still centered over your right foot as you reach and stretch your right arm upward."* (pause)

Step 8. *"Notice if your breathing changes as you stretch. . . . How does your body feel now? How is it different from when you were not stretching? What is the golden orb at your center doing? What does the left side of your body feel like? What is it doing?"* (pause)

Step 9. *"Now gently and slowly lower your arm and shift your weight back to both feet. What sensations are going through your body right now? How is your breathing? Your radiating orb is back to center. . . . Note to yourself how you are feeling in your body."* (pause)

Repeat the whole exercise for the left side of the body, eliminating unnecessary and repetitive instruction. It is not necessary to fully repeat steps 1–5. Begin with instructions to shift weight to the left foot [end of step 5] and continue as follows.

Step 10. *"Continue to breathe and relax as you listen. Right now, you are standing with your weight on both feet. Your center, or the place where you imagine the golden orb of light, is directly above the middle point between your two feet. Not yet, but when I tell you to shift, I want you to shift most of your weight onto the left foot. The radiating sphere of your center will then be positioned directly above your left foot and leg. Now, very gently, very slowly, shift your weight."* (pause)

Step 11. *"Most of your weight and the sphere should now both be over the left foot. Notice how this feels different from standing on both feet. . . . How does the pull of gravity feel different? Did you stop breathing as you moved? What are your right foot and leg doing right now? How do your left leg and foot feel right now? Just tune in and notice these things for a moment."* (pause)

Step 12. *"Now, continue to breathe and notice the experience of your body as you move your left arm upward until it is reaching for a spot somewhere between where the ceiling ends and the walls start. The radiating sphere is still centered over your left foot as you reach and stretch your right arm upward."* (pause)

Step 13. *"Notice if your breathing changes as you stretch. . . . How does your body feel now? How is it different from when you were not stretching? What is the golden orb at your center doing? What does the right side of your body feel like? What is it doing?"* (pause)

Step 14. *"Now gently and slowly lower your arm and shift your weight back to both feet. What sensations are going through your body right now? How is your breathing? Your radiating orb is back to center. . . . Note to yourself how you are feeling in your body."* (pause)

(After returning to center, guide participants in the final portion of the exercise.)

Step 15. *"Continue to breathe deeply and tune into the tug of gravity at your fingertips."* (pause)

Step 16. *"As you feel the tug at your fingertips, allow your head to fall forward so that your chin drops to rest upon your chest."* (pause)

Step 17. *"Slowly begin to curl your back and roll your torso over and downward as gravity continues to pull your hands and arms slowly down toward the ground."* (pause)

Step 18. *"As your body curls forward, allow your hands and arms and then your head to lead the way and go down as far as you feel comfortable doing so."* (pause)

STAND   Begin Roll   Hang   Return

Step 19. *"Allow your back to curve and, with your knees slightly bent, allow yourself to hang and feel the tension between the pull of gravity and your own balance."* (pause)

Step 20. *"Notice what this feels like in your body. . . . What has happened to your breath? Where is the glowing sphere now? What does your spine feel like curved over? What happens in your body if you stretch the hump in your spine upward toward the ceiling? What do your arms feel like as they hang downward?"* (pause)

Step 21. *"Now, very gently, very slowly, begin to uncurl and roll back upward. . . . Uncurl your spine one vertebra at a time and allow your arms and hands to trail behind and return to center at your own pace. . . . Imagine the radiating sphere moving back to your center, breathe deeply, and notice the sensations in your body as you return to center."* (pause)

(Allow participants to return to standing before the final direction.)

Step 22. *"Now, allow your focus to expand back into the room. Slowly bring yourself into the room. . . . You can begin to move and gently stretch at your own pace and, when you are ready, please return to your chairs so we can discuss the exercise."*

Spend some time discussing how this exercise was for participants. Focus on exploring what it was like to focus and tune in to the simple movements and how they felt in their bodies (i.e., what did they notice that surprised them, what was not a surprise).

■Didactic Component

How the Body Came to Be a Curse

The following questions and points should help facilitate an interactive didactic presentation of the relationship between *trauma and body image*.

Question 1: What do we mean when we say body image?
(Possible Answers: how we view our bodies; what we think about our physical appearance; judgments we make about ourselves; how attractive we are or are not; sex appeal; desirability; ideas about what we should look or be like, physically; how big, small, tall, fat, pretty, or ugly we are).
Answer 1: Body image is the view that we have in regards to our physical characteristics.

Question 2: What are some of the things that influence our opinions about our bodies?
(Possible Answers: the media, Hollywood, fashion magazines, advertising, people around us, etc.)
Answer 2: There are many factors that influence our ideas about our bodies, including our sociocultural lens as well as past experiences, which taught us how our bodies are viewed by others.

Question 3: As a result of these influences, what do some people do in order to make their body fit unreal expectations or hide the fact that they fall short of meeting unrealistic standards?
(Possible Answers: starving, hiding, over-exercising, compensating in other areas, twisting themselves into knots to be perfect, etc.)
Answer 3: People, especially women, often do many things to make up for falling short of what is considered the standard of beauty.

Question 4: If many women generally struggle with distorted views of body image as influenced by the lens through which our society judges worth and beauty, how might the same struggle for survivors of trauma and abuse be even more difficult and complex? (Hint: Think about the Triadic Self!!!!)

(Possible Answers: survivors carry an extra burden of shame; survivors have learned to hate their bodies for far deeper reasons; the body is the very reminder of the abuse, the body is a curse because it got you in trouble in the first place, etc.)

Answer 4: Survivors of trauma and abuse have the added distortion of viewing themselves through the lens of the Triadic Self (i.e., the Abuser, the Victim, and the Nonprotecting Bystander).

Question 5: Like women who are influenced to do things to their bodies to match society's view of what they should be, survivors are influenced to do things to their bodies that match the distorted view of the Triadic Self. What messages does the Triadic Self send to the victim regarding his or her body? *On the board, write Abuser, Victim, and Nonprotecting Bystander in 3 columns and have group members generate a list.*

Answer 5:

Abuser	Victim	Nonprotecting Bystander
Your body is not your own!	My body is dirty!	I can't protect your body!
Your body needs to be punished!	My body damaged!	I don't care about your body!
Your body is worthless!	My body has betrayed me!	There is nothing I can do to help you!

Question 6: These messages may have influenced how some of you view your body. As a result, these messages may also have influenced how you treat your body. In what ways have you responded to these messages about your body?
(Possible Answers: I poison it with drugs and alcohol; I hide it or make it ugly so no one will want to touch it; I pad it for protection; I wound it by cutting and burning myself; I leave it whenever I can; I try and make it perfect so no one will hurt it, etc.)

Answer 6: Each of you probably has different ways of acting on the distorted view of your body that was passed on to you by your experience of trauma or abuse. The thing to do now is to remove the distorted lens and begin to see yourself and your body with new clarity!

KEY POINTS TO REMEMBER

Body image can become distorted by experiences of trauma or abuse.

As a result, survivors often view their bodies through the distorted lens of the Triadic Self.

Survivors may view and treat their bodies in abusive, nonprotecting, and victimizing ways.

The distortions they hold about their bodies are lies told to them by the Triadic Self. They need to gently take off the distorted lens they have worn for so long and slowly begin to see their bodies as "gifts."

■ Process Component

Gaining Clarity: Looking Through a New Lens

Invite the participants to respond to the following process questions in dyads.

1. What is your favorite body part and why?
2. What is the strongest part of your body and why?
3. What is a special thing that your body can do!
4. Name at least one (if not more) positive, nurturing things your body likes best.

When the full group reforms, invite the dyad members to share each others' responses to the questions above.

■ Experiential Component

HELPFUL HINT
The didactic portion of this group should flow smoothly into the Process Component.

The Body Is a Gift

This exercise should begin to transform negative ideas about one's body into more positive and healthy ones. The body is indeed a miraculous gift that we carry with us all of the time. This exercise is designed to increase participants' awareness of this gift and the need for them to value, treasure, and care for it. Use the following guidelines to direct the exercise; put relevant instructions on the board.

HELPFUL HINTS
Have an assortment of boxes, wrapping paper, construction paper, markers, and pens easily accessible.

Have blank cards available for the second half of the exercise.

Step 1. *"I want you to pretend you are putting together the makings of a very special and wondrous gift—the gift of your body. The first thing to do is to consider how your body is this very special and amazing gift. What do you value about having a body? What do you value about your body? What is precious and special about being able to move and breathe and think and do all the things you can do? What are the things you love and are grateful for about your body? What are the things you want for your body?*

"Using the materials at hand, you can write letters, draw pictures, write words on bits of paper or cut out shapes to symbolize all the things that make your body a gift. Think of the things you value about having a body as well as the amazing capacities and abilities of your own body and what makes it a special one. Fill the boxes before you with these items."

Step 2. *"After you have named all the things you want to include, carefully write a list of instructions on how to care for this very special gift."*

Step 3. *"Once you are done, seal up the box and pass it to the person you partnered up with earlier. That person is responsible for wrapping your gift and presenting it to you with a card that says the following 'This is a very special gift. Tend it carefully. It has been wounded in the past but has a miraculous capacity for healing and resilience. It needs to be loved and cared for. It will be with you for life. Enjoy it!' "*

Allow some time at the end of the exercise for participants to exchange gifts and to talk about what this experience was like. Encourage participants to take these boxes home with them and keep them in a visible place as a reminder of the value of their bodies.

■ Maintenance

Taking Care of the Details: Treating Your Body as if It Is Something You Care About!

Many survivors of trauma and abuse have great difficulty caring for their bodies. Encourage participants to take small steps and attend to small concerns to start. Invite group members to make a self-care list of things they want to attend to in regards to their body and physical well-being. The list may include things such as making dental, OB-GYN, or other medical appointments; getting a haircut; showering daily; flossing; breast self-examination; etc. Have them identify things they can attend to over time and work toward checking off their self-care list.

Touch and Intimacy

Overview for Group Leaders

Session 9 continues the module that focuses on Trauma Reenactment and the body. Both Outer and Middle Circle themes continue to guide the group process: safety, the connections between addictive behavior and initial trauma, and testing out new support among group members. Transition to the Inner Circle occurs as deeper connections are made with the traumatic past, the role of the Triadic Self is emphasized, and the healing relationships begun in the last segment of the group's work together are nurtured.

Similar to the relationship between addictions and Trauma Reenactment, there is a paradoxical dilemma for the trauma survivor struggling with issues of touch and sexuality. Self-destructive aspects of sexual activity—like unsafe sex or sex within a distressing or inappropriate relationship—may reflect the dynamics of trauma and early abuse. Trauma and early abuse may be reenacted very differently among group members. Similar to drug and alcohol abuse, some individuals may reenact the feeling of shameful arousal they experienced during their abuse, while others may reproduce the numbness of the childhood abuse experience by being unable to experience any kind of feeling during sexual interactions. And some may use sex to place themselves in risky circumstances that reenact the danger and fear of the initial trauma. Others may use sex, like drugs or alcohol, to create the altered state or feeling of being out-of-control that they have experienced before, during, or after the abuse. Still others may reenact self-harming behavior, such as hurting themselves or others as part of their sexual activities. And some, as part of their Trauma Reenactment, will experience sexual addiction, remaining in abusive relationships that in turn mimic their childhood relationships with the abusers and non-protective bystanders. Whether the sexual reenactments are at the numbed out or the intense end of the spectrum, the self-destructive sexual patterns—colored by shame, fear, anger, and self-hatred—often feel like a reexperiencing of trauma and abuse.

Like substance use, sexual activities and fantasies are often rooted in efforts to soothe the 3-D distress that follows in the wake of trauma and abuse. Despite the pain and shame that may be present, sex can certainly feel like a solution that works. Discomfort and pain can be experienced as a necessary part of reliving the compulsive trauma memories. Some sexual reenactments may be experienced as a attempt to achieve mastery over memories: The former victim now experiences herself as in control of the discomfort. Similar to the function of substance abuse, sexual activities and fantasies can numb or amplify intense feelings, silence over-whelming negative thoughts, and distract the hopelessness of the spirit. Unfortunately, the "remedy" of sexual addiction, or sexually distressing activities and fantasies, becomes an unbearable source of shame: Sex becomes the "abuser" and the cycle of reenactment continues over and over again.

Group Leaders' Tasks for Session 9

Group leaders should facilitate the following group processes:

- Guided Relaxation Exercise and Check-In: relaxation response practice, check-in, and brief review of the Trauma Reenactment, Triadic Self, and Protective Presence concepts.
- Process Component: facilitate reflection and exploration of themes involving sexual addictions as Trauma Reenactment; recognize problems associated with intimacy and touch and barriers to healing and recovery.
- Didactic Component: present information on the relationship between Trauma Reenactment, addictions, and sexual issues.
- Experiential Component: group creation of the Triadic Self's negative messages regarding physical intimacy; creating a healing Protective Presence through the use of music, healing gestures, and the creation of new messages.
- Maintenance: identify positive sources of comfort and healing components of the Protective Presence through lists, image-making, and music.

Group Leaders' Pre-Group Preparation for Session 9

1. Bring post-it notes for Part I of this session's experiential component.
2. Review the Protective Presence exercise in Session 3 on pp. 71–74 for Part II of this session's experiential component.

3. Make copies of the rating exercise to distribute to the group.

Group Member Goals for Session 9

Group members should achieve the following goals:

- understand the relationship between sex and Trauma Reenactment
- identify (1) how their own issues with touch and sexual expression reenacts their own experience of trauma and (2) barriers to healing regarding safe touch and sex
- begin the process of creating new experiences of touch and safety in sexual expression through working with the expanded Protective Presence

■ Guided Relaxation Exercise and Check-In

In this week's check-in, after the opening relaxation exercise, group leaders should check in with participants about their ongoing relaxation response practice. Use the following questions as guidelines.

→ How did the new idea of your body as a "gift" influence your week?
→ How often were you able to do your relaxation response practice?
→ What did you notice about your practice this week?
→ How have you found the practice to be helpful or difficult over the past week?

Facilitators should also present a very brief review of Trauma Reenactment and the Triadic Self in relation to issues of body image and encourage the sharing of questions, insights, and reflections that may have arisen over the past week. Be sure to emphasize the following central points during the review.

- *Trauma Reenactment* occurs when trauma and abuse from the past is carried forward into your life today and is "reenacted" by self-destructive behaviors and ways of thinking about yourself.
- *Trauma Reenactment* creates 3-D Distress—this distress relating to physical intimacy and sexuality affects the mind, body, and spirit.
- *Trauma Reenactment*—especially in regard to sexuality—manifests differently for different people.
- *The Triadic Self* comprises the three internalized parts of the self: Abuser, Victim, and Nonprotecting Bystander. This is an internal reenactment of the trauma and of being abused and not being protected. The two steps to

healing are (1) to identify these three parts of the self when a cycle of self-harmful activity is happening and (2) to replace the Triadic Self with a strong Protective Presence.

■Process Component

Encourage group members to respond to the following questions in a "brainstorming" format; answers should be fairly brief and spontaneous.

In what ways, in general, does abuse have an impact on:

- non-sexual touch?
- sexual fantasies?
- sexual closeness?
- sexual activities?
- sexual risk-taking?
- sexual partners? (who they are . . . how many . . .)

Potential answers might include:

- recreates feelings of shame
- recreates feelings of fear or revulsion
- recreates a sense of danger, risk, fear, heightened arousal
- recreates an out-of-control feeling
- recreates feelings of worthlessness, hopelessness, despair, isolation
- makes it easier to engage in other self-destructive reenacting behaviors like violence, use of addictions, cutting, burning, etc.
- keeps people stuck in abusive reenacting relationships
- recreates feelings of disconnection from others

Rating Exercise

Invite each person to rate the following in private—provide paper and pencils. On a scale of 1–5, how comfortable or uncomfortable are you with:

- Non-sexual closeness (hugs, affection, touching of any kind)
- Sexual closeness
- Sexual fantasies
- Choice of sexual partners
- Sexual activities

■Didactic Component

It is important to remind the group of how their own addictions and sexuality serve as both **self-destructive** reenactments and misguided efforts to **self-soothe** 3-D distress. Encourage participants to use the handouts during the Didactic Component and to make notes.

Key Points

1. Most survivors of trauma or early abuse have a variety of challenges attached to physical intimacy, whether it is nonsexual affection or sexual activities and situations. Like the addictions involving alcohol, drugs, food, or self-injury, distressing sexual behaviors or addictions may serve to—at least temporarily—soothe our 3-D distress, thus creating a paradox not unlike the paradox we discussed in Session 3 about addictions.

2. Healthy expressions of both sexual and non-sexual physical closeness are often attempts to seek healing. Physical intimacy may be another way to respond to our experience of traumatic abuse, an effort to find the closeness or sense of specialness longed for in childhood.

3. In an effort to deal with your addiction and your experience of trauma, many treatment interventions or self-healing efforts have been frustrating, leaving a feeling of emptiness and shame. Sometimes we try to find healing through physical closeness and sexual experiences so that we can feel that we are in control of our bodies and our choice to be physical with someone, whether or not we are actually in control or in charge. So it is not surprising that sex and other forms of physical closeness can get very complicated for many trauma survivors.

Here are some reasons we may have difficulties with sex or physical closeness.

-   The current experience of touch may replicate the abusive touch from the past.
-   Sexual activities or fantasies may activate painful memories.
-   Sexual activities or fantasies may recreate old feelings of shame and self-blame.
-   Any form of physical closeness may trigger unbearable longings for comforting, healing touch, which is perhaps not matched by the person we are being touched by.
-   Sexual activities or fantasies may trigger fear or rage, including fearful and rageful feelings towards ourselves.

- In our reenactment of trauma, physical closeness or sex may be a vehicle to replay all aspects of the Triadic Self:

For example: *If I feel aroused by my sexual feelings—either in actual sexual activity or in sexual fantasies—I may feel an immediate rush of self-hate or fear. This may be because part of me feels aroused but also feels the fearfulness of the inner Victim in response to the arousal feelings. When this happens, the feelings of being aroused are reminiscent of the Abuser. When I feel like I can't stop what is happening to me—either in reality or in fantasy—then the Nonprotecting Bystander gets triggered.*

■ Experiential Component

Part I: Identifying Old Messages

Invite group members to write messages that they have received from their internalized Abusers, Victims, and Nonprotecting Bystanders on post-it notes. These messages will be about their sexual selves, about touch, or about physical closeness. Remind group members that they should do this exercise as spontaneously as possible without editing what comes to mind. They can put the post-its onto the posterboard whenever they are ready. Have one or two group members read all of these messages aloud.

Part II: Creating New Experiences

How do we begin to change these internal negative messages? Participants need to practice the process of *taking in* or *internalizing* positive, self-nurturing, protective images, connections, and relationships. The Protective Presence is reintroduced here in order to provide participants with an opportunity to continue the process of creating healthy and self-promoting internal resources of safety, self-

GROUP BRAINSTORM QUESTION

As a review, when you hear the word "protective," what words and images come to mind?

HELPFUL HINTS

The Group Brainstorm should be done at a rapid-fire pace. Encourage participants to be brief in describing their ideas and images.

Practice the Protective Presence exercise with music several times on your own so that your transitions will be smooth and fluid.

acceptance, and soothing. This supportive internalized resource can then serve as a healthy alternative to the 3-D distress that is triggered by current situations involving physical intimacy.

Note the following to participants: "*The purpose of this exercise is to help you continue to create a positive, self-nurturing, and protective resource of your own that you can call upon in times of 3-D distress when you are having trouble with touch or sexuality. Just like we did before, we are going to develop internal images of protection and self-acceptance* (insert here words and images that participants identified earlier), *and we will begin by the cultivation of an internalized Protective Presence.*"

■Group Leaders' Instructions for the Protective Presence Exercise

Step 1. Invite participants to get into comfortable and relaxed, but alert, positions in their seats.

Step 2. Say the following: "*In just a few minutes, I am going to put on some music you have heard before. It is a very soothing piece of music, as you may remember from the last time we listened to it as an invitation to explore our internal Protective Presence. We will play this particular piece of music three different times. The first time we play this music, I simply want you to listen. We will all remain seated throughout this exercise. I want those who feel comfortable doing so, to close their eyes. If you are uncomfortable closing your eyes, just let your gaze fall in a soft focus on the floor a foot or two ahead of you.*"

Step 3. Continue the explanation: "*The second time you hear the music, I want you to begin to move on your own and to create your own gestures; these can include holding your own hand, caressing your own cheek, hugging yourself, spreading your arms wide, rocking gently, or just being still and breathing deeply.*

"*The movements you choose should be ones that call forth the images or ideas you noted earlier in the brainstorming session. They should be whatever works best and are most soothing for you.*"

Step 4: Continue with the explanation: "*The third time you hear the music, I will invite you to move into the most comforting position, movement, or gesture that you have discovered. What I would like you to do is to maintain this movement throughout the entire song. If you want to change, feel free to do so. But try to stay with what you have found to be most comforting for the duration of the music.*

"*While you hold this position or movement or gesture, let your Protective Presence give you a message of self-acceptance and affirmation. Perhaps you will hear your Protective Presence tell you that you have nothing to be ashamed of. Perhaps the message will be that you are good. You are lovable. You are doing the very best that you can. You are safe and nothing can harm you.*"

Step 5. Remind group members of the following.

- *Don't worry if this sounds a bit confusing. I will lead you through it in the exercise.*
- *Breathe deeply and relax throughout the exercise.*
- *You may feel a bit self-conscious, but stay focused on yourself and on getting the most you can out of this exercise.*

Step 6. Begin the exercise by checking to make sure everyone is in a comfortable position. Begin the selected music. As it plays for the first time, remind the group to simply listen and relax. Speak in a soft and reassuring tone.

Step 7. The second time the music plays, invite participants to explore their own comforting movements and gestures that invoke images, feelings, and ideas about their own understanding of protection and safety. The movements they choose should bring feelings of safety, comfort, and soothing.

Step 8. The third time the music plays, guide the group members to move into the most comforting pattern they discovered and to gently maintain this movement, gesture, or position. Invite them to allow positive messages to emerge as they sustain these soothing movements.

Step 9: As the music fades, encourage participants to allow their focus to return to the group room at their own pace. Direct them to *gently* bring themselves back into the room, to take their time and move at their own pace.

Step 10. Allow time and space for the participants to reflect on and share their experience of this exercise.

■ Maintenance

Encourage group members to do the following and to continue with the ongoing development of a relaxation practice.

"In order to combat the negative messages we carry around inside us about touch, sex, and physical closeness, we need to create and make use of lasting sources of safety and comfort. This week, continue to identify (and write down) current positive sources of support, encouragement, comfort, and acceptance in your life. This can include everything and anything from pets to poems to music to plants and flowers to your sense of spirituality to specific friends and family. You are the expert in creating your own Protective Presence.

"Words may not be enough to describe your Protective Presence. You can also create images through drawings, collages, pictures, or favorite music. If you feel comfortable doing so, post your images and your list in a visible area of your room and refer to it

often when you might feel isolated and alone. If you have music to remind you of your Protective Presence, remember to listen to it whenever you have a few minutes."

Remind group members that three weeks remain before the group ends. Encourage them to consider how they would like to honor their healing, say farewell, and complete their process by the time they reach the last session.

Part IV

The Inner Circle

From Reenactment to Reconnection

Overview for Group Leaders

During session 10, participants will press more deeply into the Inner Circle themes. An increased sense of trust within the group has evolved over the past nine weeks, along with the individual development of skills to manage dysregulated emotion, which helps create a safe space where group members can speak more freely about their past trauma experiences. As well, the shifting frame (from victim to empowered agent of change) that has been cultivated over the past weeks gives participants a new language to speak about their experiences in terms of strength, hope, and resilience. In connecting with others, participants begin the process of connecting with the even larger community.

The fundamental and often most painful wound suffered as a result of trauma and abuse is the wound of **disconnection**—a wound that can reach deeply into the body-mind-spirit of the victim. Interpersonal trauma occurs within the context of a relationship. This traumatic relationship is clearly a distorted one and often woven with threads of shame, guilt, fear, and despair. Distorted as it may be, the traumatic relationship tends to provide a powerful "relational imprint" and can, unfortunately, definitively shape one's ideas about the meaning and expression of connection with others. A survivor's entire understanding of what a relationship is can become poisoned by the twisted meaning carried by the abusive event. As a result of early abuse or trauma, one's ability to understand the meaning of relationships and actually be *in* relationships with others may become damaged.

The serious and pervasive nature of this wound is a significant barrier to healing. Survivors live not in a vacuum but in a world that is a continual ebb and flow of relational possibilities and actualities. When trauma impairs one's ability to be in a relationship it can negatively affect one's capacity to *be in the world*. Once again, many survivors turn to alcohol and drugs to ease the discomfort of disconnection. For some, their addiction makes superficial connection tolerable. For others, addiction will feed isolation as the survivor chooses their relationship with alcohol or drugs over relationships with people. For still others, their addiction helps them maintain and manage volatile, chaotic, and self-demeaning connections. In any event, we can see the pattern of Trauma Reenactment emerge once again as addictive behavior forces the recreation of relational distortions from the early abuse.

Healing oneself by creating and exploring new, untainted connections to others *with others* is the foundation of this treatment model and the focus of this session. Participants will examine how trauma has shaped their relational capacities, how their addiction has replaced meaningful relationships, and how to move from **relational reenactment** to **relational reconnection**. Moving toward recovery from abuse as part of a process embedded in a community can go far in healing the wound of disconnection. Healing in connection can also redefine relational understanding and enhance relational capacities.

Group Leaders' Tasks for Session 10

Group leaders should facilitate the following group processes:

- Guided Relaxation Exercise and Check-In: following a brief group relaxation/mindfulness exercise, facilitators will monitor the well-being check-in done in pairs; participants will be encouraged to share responses, reflections, and insights regarding the last session on touch and sexuality.
- Experiential Component: group members will be guided to metaphorically explore the experience of connecting to and connecting with (or seeing and being seen) by others in a simple movement exercise.
- Didactic Component: myths about relationships will be identified and challenged; information will be presented on how trauma can impact the relational understanding, expression, and capacity of survivors of interpersonal violence; how traumas can lead to relational reenactment.
- Process Component: participants will examine their own patterns of relational reenactment and explore the role of addictions in relational disruption.
- Maintenance: a method of reconnecting with *the spirit* is offered.

Group Leaders' Pre-Group Preparation for Session 10

1. Select an appropriate piece of music for the experiential exercise.

Group Member Goals for Session 10

Group members should achieve the following goals:

- gain insight into the impact of trauma and abuse on relational understanding, capacity, and expression
- understand the dynamics involved in relational reenactment and be able to identify this pattern in their own lives
- understand the role that their addiction plays in cultivating disconnection and relational reenactment
- have new experiences of trust and connection that will lay the foundation for new ways of understanding relationships and seeking connection

■Guided Relaxation Exercise and Check-In

This week will have a two-part check-in. The first part will be a well-being check-in and reflection among members in groups of two. The second part will be a brief group relaxation exercise that is designed to enhance a sense of connection among group members. Begin the session by letting the group know that connection and relationship will be the central themes of this week's group.

Part A: Check-In

Instruct participants to break into pairs for a well-being check-in. Instruct them to respond to the following questions.

HELPFUL HINT
Consider writing instructions for part A on the board.

→ On a scale from 1–10, rate your overall well-being over the past week. Share with your partner why you had that rating and any steps you took to feel better.
→ Share with your partner any reflections, insights, or thoughts you have had over the past about last week's topic on touch and sexuality. What, if anything, did you do differently because of your experience in group last week?

Part B: Relaxation Exercise

Step 1. *"Please get comfortable in your chairs. We are going to do a relaxation and visualization exercise to help us increase our sense of connection to each other in the group. Please close your eyes or allow your gaze*

HELPFUL HINT
Speak slowly—pause between phrases to allow time for the group members to deepen their relaxation.

to fall in a soft focus on the floor ahead of you and turn your focus inward to your breath."

Step 2. "Allow your breath to deepen and slow down—focus on releasing and relaxing . . . allowing the concerns of the day to fall away . . . allowing yourself this time and space right now to be still and quiet and at peace."

Step 3. "Continue to allow your breath to flow in through your nose and out through your mouth. . . . Breathe deeply in . . . and deeply out . . . like the ebb and flow of waves against the shore . . . releasing, relaxing, and letting go . . . allowing waves of peace to wash gently over you."

Step 4. "As you continue to relax, allow your focus to shift from an internal focus on your breath to an external one. I want you to focus on your breath as it moves out of you and expands into the room."

Step 5. "Imagine your breath as a white vaporous cloud moving out into the room as you release it. As you release your breath, picture it floating away from you and mixing with the breath of those around you."

Step 6. "As you inhale, imagine that you are taking in the shared energy of those around you. Imagine drawing strength from the energy of everyone's collected breath, see how your breath connects you to everyone in the room."

Step 7. "Continue to breathe deeply in and deeply out, becoming aware of how the breath connects us all . . . the breath, our breath, simple and profound, is the ribbon of life that weaves us all together."

Step 8. "Imagine our collective breath as a ribbon that gently surrounds us and holds us together in our efforts toward recovery and healing."

Step 9. "Breathing deeply in, we are connected . . . releasing our breath, we connect."

Step 10. "Allow yourself a few moments to revel in this collective connection, feeling safe, restful, relaxed, and feeling at peace." (pause)

Step 11. "At your own pace, gently bring your focus back in to the room . . . and open your eyes when you feel ready."

■Experiential Component

HELPFUL HINTS

Group leaders should always read through the experiential exercises prior to the session so that transitions and instructions are fluid.

Select an appropriate piece of music—either an instrumental piece or an appropriate (i.e., with themes of connection, reflection, etc.) vocal piece.

Group leaders should participate and model the exercise in case participants feel unsure or at a loss as to what to do.

Monitor and guide the group during the process. Offer encouragement and suggestions for movement when appropriate.

"Mirror, Mirror . . ."

This exercise is designed to allow participants to connect with other group members in a nonverbal manner. As all attempts to connect with others involve some risk, this experiential activity was developed to minimize interpersonal risk. Reassure participants that if the exercise becomes too uncomfortable, they should slow down or stop and then reengage at their own pace.

Step 1. Depending on available space, this exercise can be done sitting or standing. If space is available, ask participants to stand, move their chairs out of the center of the room, and find a partner. If the space is too small, have participants turn their chairs to face a partner and remain seated.

Step 2. Inform participants that the exercise is designed to explore nonverbal communication and connection. Explain that, in a few moments, you will begin to play some music. Reassure them that the music will not be fast-paced and no one is expected to dance. This exercise is simply about moving and connecting.

Step 3. Before you begin the music, instruct participants to turn and face each other at a comfortable distance. This comfort zone may need to be negotiated between partners, which is perfectly okay and expected. Leaders should encourage participants to ask each other what is comfortable.

Step 4. Have partners designate who will lead first and who will follow. Reassure them that everyone will get to do both so it is just a matter of deciding who will do what first. Continue to reassure the group if they begin to get anxious.

Step 5. When the music begins, the designated leader should slowly begin to move. The follower is to then follow the leader's movements or someone in the group *like a mirror image*. Demonstrate this with your co-leader or someone in the group. If the leader slowly raises their right arm out to the side, the follower will do the same, but with the left arm as if both are standing in front of a mirror. Briefly demonstrate a range of simple movements, gestures, and steps so that the group understands the exercise.

Step 6. Tell them that the leaders need to pay close attention to their partners to make sure they are following their lead, and followers need to attend to the leaders and do their best to reflect the movement that is presented to them.

Step 7. Halfway through the exercise, you will say "switch" and partners will reverse roles (i.e., leaders will follow and followers will lead).

Step 8. Encourage participants to expand the movements as they do the exercise and begin to feel more comfortable with their partner. Also, encourage them to monitor how they are feeling during the exercise and to notice how or when this feeling does (or does not) change.

Step 9. Before you start the music, ask the group if they have any questions about the exercise. Continue to assuage any concerns and reaffirm a sense of safety for the group by letting them know they can go at their own pace. Inform group members that many of the feelings they are having at this very moment may, in fact, be reflections of old relational patterns—they may be anxious, scared, intimidated, or fearful of appearing stupid or awkward. Therefore, encourage them to take this opportunity to experiment with connecting to others in a new way. Validate that they may feel awkward at first, but that they should try to allow their concerns to fall away for the moment and engage themselves fully in the exercise.

Step 10. As the music begins, encourage participants to start moving slowly. As they begin to feel more comfortable with each other, direct them to experiment with new movement ideas while always maintaining a nonverbal connection with their partner.

Step 11. Encourage participants as needed throughout the exercise as you and your co-leader model the exercise at the front of the room. Halfway through the music, tell the participants to switch. Prompt them to tune into how their feelings may have changed when they changed roles.

Step 12. At the end of the exercise, have members return to their seats. Lead a group discussion on how the exercise went. Explore the following issues: how their feelings did or did not change; their experience of nonverbal connection and communication; issues of trust that may have arisen during the exercise; what was fun; what was hard; what it was like to tune into someone else in this way; what it felt like to switch; how the exercise may have related to any particular individual issues that participants may have revealed earlier in the session.

■Didactic Component

Building Connections: Barriers to Healing

In the introduction to the didactic portion, discuss distorted beliefs or myths about relationships, such as all-or-nothing thinking patterns, inaccuracies, misconceptions, etc., that may have emerged for the group members as a result of trauma or abuse. These same myths will be challenged in light of new information provided later in this section.

HELPFUL HINTS

Generate suggestions from the group for the section on myths.

Refer to the Overview section to supplement the talking points section.

Use the talking points as discussion guidelines.

Myths about Relationships and Connection

Generate a list of possible beliefs or myths on the board with the group that participants may believe as a result of their experience with interpersonal trauma. As a facilitator, you might suggest and include some of the following myths.

Myth #1: All relationships hurt.

Myth #2: All relationships are supposed to hurt.

Myth #3: I am too damaged to be in a relationship with anybody.

Myth #4: Real relationships are for everyone else but me.

Myth #5: I can't trust anyone (or I trust everybody).

Myth #6: I am powerless in my relationship.

Myth #7: I was meant to be alone in the world.

Myth #8: I can be with anybody and everybody I want.

Myth #9: I do/don't care about other people.

Myth #10: I'm scared I'm so screwed up, I will hurt someone.

Myth #11: I can/cannot control what other people do to me.

Myth #12: It's not my fault other people feel hurt by what I do.

Myth #13: I am nothing and nobody without a relationship.

Leave these myths on the board as you begin the following presentation on how trauma impacts one's understanding of relationships, expression of connection, and capacity to be in a relationship. Use the following key talking points to guide the presentation.

Talking Point #1

The most painful wound suffered as a result of interpersonal violence and trauma is often the wound of disconnection.

- Trauma often happens in the context of a relationship.
- The traumatic relationship can provide a powerful and distorted imprint of what relationships mean and how they are expressed.
- Survivors can take in this distortion and may begin to believe that the distortion is in fact the truth.
- This chain of events can lead to deeply imbedded but inaccurate beliefs about relationships, an inaccurate understanding of the meaning of connection, and an impaired capacity to be in healthy relationships. This all creates *the wound of disconnection*.

Talking Point #2

This relational wound may show up in many relational ways. It can:

- distort ideas about and damage the capacity for trust
- create relationship boundaries that are too rigid, too flexible, or too variable
- create difficulty with commitment
- lead to a fear of, and difficulty with, intimacy

- lead to abusive, chaotic, unpredictable relationships
- contribute to unfulfilling, meaningless relationships
- influence self-sabotaging, passive, or aggressive behavior in relationships

Elicit other ideas from the group.

Talking Point #3

The initial traumatic relationship can become internalized as the Triadic Self. Remember that the Triadic Self is not so much about internalizing the *roles* of Abuser, Victim, and Nonprotecting Bystander, but about internalizing the *relationship* among the three.

- These negative relational models from the past may unfortunately influence and guide an individual's current relational patterns. This is *relational reenactment.*
- When survivors examine their current relationships and connections over time with family, friends, intimates, and co-workers, a pattern of relational reenactment often emerges.
- Survivors often never feel safe or really feel connected to others because they have never internalized a positive, protective relationship. *(Emphasize this point!!!!)*

Talking Point #4

How do addictions fit into this picture of relational disconnection? Drugs, alcohol, or food can serve as poor substitutes for connection; they may be seen as misguided efforts to increase connection or facilitate relational reenactment.

- Many addicts and alcoholics abandon relationships with others that are too overwhelming or difficult to manage for a relationship with the addictive behavior of their choice.
- Many use their addiction to ease their social discomfort and to try to make connection easier or more tolerable.
- The self-destructive nature of addiction serves as another means for the cycle of Trauma Reenactment to play out in a survivor's life.

Concluding Points

(Refer back to the list of myths.) *"If we reexamine these myths, we can see that all of them are rooted in a false premise or that the assumptions the myths are based upon are false. Lies about what relationships are and how to negotiate them emerge from the dis-*

torted relational imprint of trauma and are played out in the cycle of Trauma Reenactment." (Take a moment to challenge the myths presented. Validate the participants' experiences of these myths as being true, but also guide them toward other ways of understanding and experiencing relationships.)

- We need to come to terms with the idea that how we have understood and expressed ourselves relationally may have been tainted by our experiences of abuse and trauma.
- In doing this, we can acknowledge and experience other ways of understanding and expressing connection and challenge these myths and beliefs that have kept us from being relationally free.
- Also, our relational capacity can expand and the wound of disconnection can heal. We can move from relational reenactment to relational reconnection by creating healing connections.

■Process Component

Uncovering Personal Myths and Discovering New Meanings

Use the following questions to guide the process discussion.

1. What are your biggest barriers to or fears of connection?
2. How is your addiction like a relationship? (i.e., it is always there, I can always count on it, it never leaves me alone, it comforts me, it makes me feel better, it's dependable, it does not judge me, it hurts me, it betrays me, etc.)
3. How have you used your addiction to manage disconnection?
4. How have you connected with others despite your experience of relational wounding?
5. Name some ways you can begin to overcome your barriers to connection.

HELPFUL HINT
Be aware that this section covers considerably more material than those in previous sessions. Allow enough time for this. The nature of the topic demands the expansion of discussion, sharing, and communication among the entire group. It is designed to help facilitate reconnection with others by beginning with connecting to other group members.

■Maintenance

Reconnecting with the Self

Invite group members to engage in the following exploration on their own.

- *Make a list of all the qualities that you admire in someone you would want to have a connection with. (Include qualities such as integrity, dependability, loyalty, patience, tolerance, etc.)*
- *Now add the word self in front of each of these.*
- *Over time, intentionally begin to cultivate these qualities within yourself.*
- *As you do so, your connection to yourself and your spirit and others will grow!*

■Special Instruction

Group leaders should ask group members to bring an object to the next session that represents a favorite healing outdoor setting.

Environmental Healing: Spirit in Community

Overview for Group Leaders

This is an important part of the central task of the Inner Circle—the reworking of the trauma. Although all sessions have addressed aspects of trauma's impact on the spirit as well as the mind and body, this is the only session devoted primarily to the healing of the spirit. It is also the only session that includes bringing aspects of Nature into the session and the possibility of meeting outdoors.

Group leaders should be aware that few traditional models specifically address the centrality of spirituality in recovery although most people who have experienced childhood would agree that trauma creates major challenges in terms of the survivor's **spiritual well-being**. The 12-step programs for addictions are a notable exception because the connection to one's Higher Power is considered essential to helping people achieve recovery from their addictions. However, most mental health professionals are trained to separate spiritual healing from mental and physical health practices. The ATRIUM model considers healing the spirit as important as healing the body and mind. This may seem surprising—and maybe even a little uncomfortable at first—for any group leaders (and group members) who have focused recovery efforts within the confines of the traditional medical model of healing.

The ATRIUM model views spiritual distress as a breakdown in connection with the larger community, as well as a feeling of pervasive despair, an unwilling-ness to trust, and a breakdown of faith. "Spirit" may simply mean fellowship, love, and friendship. Or the word may mean, for some, a relationship with God, Goddess, Higher Power, or perhaps Nature. However it is described, it is a process through which complete healing equals *renewed hope* by reconnecting with a supportive community.

In this session, group leaders encourage group members to make healing connections with each other and with nonhuman sources of support (pets, plants, Nature). Through these potentially less threatening nonpower-based relationships, a renewed faith in a loving community may repair shattered trust and faith. In many indigenous cultures, healing from emotional or mental problems involves primary input from spiritual healers, just as many of these cultures have never separated healing the mind from healing the body! These cultures also believe that healing connections with one's environment is central to healing the mind, body, and spirit. Learning from their beliefs, we move the setting of healing in session 11 to the outdoor environment and emphasize the reworking of the trauma story through the lens of a deepening spiritual rootedness.

Group Leaders' Tasks for Session 11

Group leaders should facilitate the following group processes:

- Check-In: if you are planning to take the group outdoors, make sure everyone is ready to move to whatever outdoor setting the group leaders have chosen for the beginning of the session; if not, proceed with customary breathing meditation.
- Process Component: facilitate reflection and exploration of connections between the natural environment and each individual's experience of well-being, adventure, and healing; explore barriers to healing and recovery in Nature; invite group members to share what they have brought in to represent their outdoor experience (see Maintenance instructions at the end of session 10).
- Didactic Component: present information on the relationship between Trauma Reenactment and distress of the spirit.
- Experiential Component: creation of healing through guided "safe space" meditation using whatever group members have brought into session with them to represent a connection with Nature.
- Maintenance: identify positive sources of comfort and healing in each person's natural environment; instructions for "gifts" group members will bring to session 12 to celebrate finishing their work together.

Group Member Goals for Session 11

Group members should achieve the following goals:

- understand the relationship between spiritual disconnections and Trauma Reenactment
- identify: (1) how to access aspects of spiritual renewal through connections with natural environment and play and (2) barriers to spiritual healing in connection to Nature
- create new experiences of well-being, play, and peacefulness through (1) working with the expanded Protective Presence and (2) a deepened understanding of the internally constructed safe place

■Check-In

HELPFUL HINTS

Before the session, choose an outdoor setting not far from where the group usually meets.

Make sure that there are no accessibility problems, so that all group members may move comfortably and easily in the area you have chosen.

Make sure the space is safe—with no foreseeable threats from human or animal predators.

Pick a cleared area so that all members of group are within seeing and hearing distance.

Be prepared to use "Plan B" in case of bad weather.

Plan A—Going Outdoors

Group leaders should check-in with participants regarding their readiness to move outdoors (i.e., are they dressed appropriately for the climate and terrain, etc.). Any worries, fears, or hesitations should be addressed briefly, although leaders should try to be as optimistic and relaxed about this venture as possible. Reassure the group that you feel comfortable with the environment they will be exploring, and that no one will have to stay any longer outdoors than they are comfortable. Remind the group that they will stay outdoors for only part of the session and return to the meeting room shortly.

Plan B—Staying Indoors

You may need to use this alternative in case of very bad weather, if a group member is legitimately unable to go outdoors, or if liability issues preclude taking the group outside the building. Begin the session with relaxation meditation, as usual. You can plan a longer time and then remind the group that they are now able to focus on their breathing and meditation practice for a longer period of time than when they first began the group.

■Process Component

Plan A

When you are in the outdoor space with the group, encourage group members to move away from each other but to remain visible to each other. Suggest that each person move into a space that attracts them (perhaps near a tree or looking at a special view of the sky) and stay still for five minutes.

Say the following to the group: *"As you stay quietly in your chosen space, notice the sounds, the smells, the textures, the ways in which you feel more alive in your body, mind, and spirit. Notice if you are breathing deeply, and notice if the space allows you to feel relaxed in your body."*

At the end of the five minutes, ask the group to either stand in a circle or, if it is comfortable, to sit down on the ground and briefly share their experience, reminding them of the instructions you suggested at the beginning of the exercise.

Their answers might include: feelings of initial anxiety or discomfort; wondering if others had chosen a "better" space; experiencing the sounds of Nature (i.e. birds, wind, insects, dogs), alongside manmade sounds; connecting sensual experiences like sun, breeze, moisture with emotions—for example, "The sun made me feel happy," "The breeze made me feel nervous or alive."

After this brief sharing exercise, ask each group member to find something to bring back to the meeting room that reminds them of something they have just experienced.

Plan B

In this alternative, the Process Component is the time for group members to share the object they brought with them to represent their outdoor experience. Each group member should be invited to show the object (or picture of a scene representing the place they chose) and tell the group briefly about what the place was like and what it means to them.

■Didactic Component

"Survivors of trauma or abuse frequently have a variety of challenges related to spiritual well-being. Today, we are working towards a new understanding of spiritual connectedness through our exploration of healing in relation to Nature."

A. Ask group to brainstorm what they mean by "spiritual well-being." Suggest that they broaden the definition to include examples like feeling trust in the universe, harmony with Nature, and safety and a place of belonging in the human community.

B. Here are some reasons for why we may have trouble feeling spiritual well-being:

- past experiences of religious institutions or leaders that included replications of abuse and non-protection
- authority figure or religious "rules" and judgments may activate painful, shameful, or angry feelings and flashbacks
- spiritual activities or wishes for spiritual connection may recreate feelings of hopelessness and self-blame
- the desire to experience trust and a rightful place of safety in the human community—or the universe—may trigger unbearable longings for comfort and healing that are not met by the human or spiritual communities we are approaching
- attempts to feel spiritual connection through Nature-based activities may trigger fear or sometimes even actual experiences of discomfort or being unsafe

■Experiential Component

HELPFUL HINTS

Play soothing music with this relaxation exercise.

Allow participants to choose between closing their eyes and focusing externally on an object.

Inform participants of the nature of the exercise in advance.

Invite all participants to hold the reminder of the time just spent outdoors during this exercise. You might suggest that they think of this item as something that will most reflect the "safe haven" they will create in their imaginations.

Have a range of other items for participants to choose from such as rocks, flowers, or leaves, in case some of them have not found something to bring back from the recent outdoor component of the session.

Remind the group how the relaxation response and the creation-of-safe-space visualization exercises have already helped to manage hyperarousal and anxiety. The following repetition of the safe space exercise is designed to guide participants in grounding themselves in a safe place using the connection with Nature as a way to practice their deepening practice of spiritual well-being.

Step 1. Have participants begin with the relaxation response.

Step 2. Next, ask them to visualize a place outdoors where they feel safe and unafraid. This can be an outdoor space near their home/apartment/ room, a sandy beach, a deep forest, or even snuggled in a favorite chair looking outside at the sky—wherever they feel safe and unafraid.

Step 3. Invite the group members to imagine this scene as vividly as possible, to create it in specific detail in their imaginations. Have them imagine the colors that are present in the setting, the textures, smells, sounds, sensations, etc. Guide their efforts in painting the scene vividly in their mind's eye by suggesting different possibilities (i.e., Are there animals in your scene? What are they doing? Is there a breeze? What are the things you smell in your safe place?)

Step 4. Once the scene has been created, invite participants to enter the scene and imagine what they are doing, feeling, and thinking as they move about or stay still. Offer neutral cues to guide the participants' efforts (i.e., Is there a breeze? Can you feel it against your skin? Is your space sunny and warm? Can you feel the earth against your body?)

Step 5. Allow participants to remain silent in their scene for several minutes before inviting them to return to the room at their own pace.

Step 6. Spend a few minutes processing the experience with the group. See how they connect their visualization with their outdoor experience. Inform the group members that they can go to this safe place anytime they choose. It is the choosing which makes this a powerful experience rather than the particular details of the safe space. This safe space may even change from time to time.

Reminder: Part of developing a sense of spiritual well-being involves integrating the concept of the Protective Presence in regular visualization, meditation, and prayer. Their Protective Presence is connected to their spiritual well-being just as much as their work to develop a safe space.

■Maintenance

"Making connections with each other, the environment, and the safe space and Protective Presence within, all require practice. This week, do each of the following at least once:

- *Reach out in some way to another group member.*
- *Try going outdoors for at least 10 minutes and explore ways to make your connection to Nature a healing activity for your spirit.*

- *Spend at least ten minutes visualizing your safe space—remember to relax your body through mindful breathing and tension reduction skills.*
- *Spend some time getting in touch with your Protective Presence."*

Reminder: Next week is the final group meeting. Encourage the participants to bring something that inspires them (i.e., a poem, a picture, etc.) to the session next week. Finally, ask the group members to think about what they may want to say in the letter that they will write to future group participants in the final session.

The Journey
toward Hope

Overview for Group Leaders

In this final session, the Inner Circle themes open and expand outward as participants end their journey and move back into their everyday lives. By utilizing all that they have learned, group members have the opportunity to generate a healing bridge to the larger community; this would be a bridge that carries survivors of interpersonal violence and abuse out of the devastating cycle of Trauma Reenactment and into a new and powerful way of living in the world.

This session guides participants in weaving together the threads of their experiences over the past 12 weeks in the hope of creating a healing tapestry they can carry with them. They have been introduced to new ideas and new ways of thinking about their past. It is important to review these ideas against the larger backdrop of cultivating balance and alleviating 3-D distress in the mind-body-spirit triad. They have learned a new language of hope, resilience, and strength. This provides them with an opportunity to express themselves and their understanding of their experiences, in these new ways in a context of safety, connection, and validation. They have learned to hope once again—hope for a life not dominated by their early experience of trauma and abuse. Foster their hope and encourage their ongoing efforts to maintain the positive gains and regenerative changes they have made. Allow participants to say goodbye in the way that best honors their own healing experience.

Group Leaders' Tasks for Session 12

Group leaders should facilitate the following group processes:

- Guided Relaxation Exercise and Check-In: lead group in a brief well-being check-in; discuss insights and gains made from last week's session on the environment.
- Didactic Component: review through a Q & A discussion the topics covered over the past 12 weeks, discuss resources that group members may want to use for themselves in their continued healing process.
- Process Component: facilitate examination of gains and benefits as well as difficulties of the entire group process; explore both what worked and what did not work and what could be done to make the process better. Also identify the most significant gains participants have made in their lives over the past three months.
- Experiential Component: invite participants to engage in an experiential exercise designed to facilitate connection and continuity with the larger healing community through (1) inviting group members to share objects, poems, pictures, stories they have brought to session today in celebration of the group's meaning for them; (2) directing group members to write brief letters to women who will be in future ATRIUM groups.
- Maintenance: encourage the ongoing practice of gains made in group.

Group Leaders' Pre-Group Preparation for Session 12

1. Bring materials for participants to write letters to the next group participants, including note paper, envelopes, and markers for drawing.
2. Prepare list of local resources, including phone numbers for 12-step groups, advocacy programs, counseling centers, volunteer services, homeless shelters, etc.

Group Member Goals for Session 12

Group members should achieve the following goals:

- ask any questions and seek clarity regarding any of the material presented over the three-month group process
- express their experience of the group process including insights, gains made, benefits, areas of improvement, gifts of poems, stories, pictures
- connect with and contribute to the larger healing community
- participate in the closing exercise of passing along their experience through letter writing

■Guided Relaxation Exercise and Check-In

Begin with the usual relaxation exercise at the start of group. Facilitate a well-being check-in for participants and encourage reflection on any progress made over the week. Use the following questions to guide the brief check-in:

→ On a scale from 1–10, how would you rate your overall well-being this week?

→ What, if any, action did you take to make your life better this week?

→ What, if any, insights or gains have you made over the past week as a result of what you learned from last week's session?

■Didactic Component

Group leaders should review past session topics. Offer a brief synopsis of each session before asking if participants have questions. Be sure to use handouts from previous sessions to facilitate this. After questions are addressed, ask participants what has been most helpful about the information and skills presented throughout the twelve sessions.

Topics

- Traumatic stress
- Trauma Reenactment
- Addictions
- Emotion regulation
- Anger
- Anxiety
- Somatization
- Body image
- Touch and intimacy
- Interpersonal relationships
- Environment and spirituality

Community Resources

The second part of the Didactic Component is the sharing of community resources. Group leaders should be prepared with phone numbers and brief descriptions of local resources that group participants may want to explore in their continuing recovery process. Typical resource information requested or needed by group participants include phone numbers for:

- 12-step groups
- domestic violence and sexual assault support services
- health care services
- counseling centers
- volunteer programs or services
- homeless shelters
- expressive arts programs
- recreational programs

Group members may also wish to share resources they have used. This is also a good time for group members to recommend written materials, music, movies, Web sites, etc., they have found helpful.

■Process Component

Group leaders should facilitate a process discussion that allows participants to explore gains and insights made over the past 12 weeks and experiences of the group process. Make sure they also have room to express their struggles as well. Use the following questions to guide the discussion and encourage them to respond along mind-body-spirit dimensions.

1. What, if any, significant insights have you made about your issues related to trauma and addictions?
2. What changes or gains, if any, have you made in your life secondary to these insights?
3. What was most helpful about the group for you?
4. What was most difficult about the group for you?

■Experiential Component

The experiential component will consist of two parts designed to deepen the connection that participants are encouraged to make with each other and with the larger community.

Letter Writing

Invite the group members to engage in the following exercise, which generates a bridge of healing from themselves to the next group of participants.

Step 1. *"We invite each of you to write a letter or note to someone in the next group. It can be anonymous if you like. The idea is to remember your own feelings as you entered this group process three months ago and think about what you wish someone had said to you at that time. You can share with them what was good, what was hard, what was useful about the group if you like. Think about what would have been most helpful for you to hear from someone when you first started on this part of your journey."*

Step 2. Allow time for the participants to both write their letters and share them with the rest of the group.

Step 3. Have participants place their letters in an envelope and seal it. Co-facilitators will then pass the letters on to the next group participants.

HELPFUL HINTS
Have materials ready in advance so time is not wasted.

Play soothing music in the background during the exercise.

Sharing of "Gifts"

Proceed with the sharing of poems, stories, pictures, and anything else brought to this last session by the participants themselves. This is the time for group members to deepen their connections with each other by offering their individual gifts of expression to reflect on what the group has meant to them. Allow enough time for this segment of the Experiential Component so that there is time for each woman to share something. Avoid interpreting or evaluating each person's gift. Often the best response is simply to thank each woman at the conclusion of her offering.

■Maintenance

Complacency and distorted thinking can sabotage the best efforts to change. Encourage participants to be alert for signs of complacency and distorted thinking in their lives that could undermine their efforts to maintain positive gains. Help them identify *early warning signals* or signs of risk that they can respond to in order to avoid falling back into a self-destructive cycle.

Some of the following thoughts can be warning signs:

- I'm better now, I can handle just one drink.
- I'm safe now/strong now and I can be around my old drinking/drugging buddies.
- I don't need to _____anymore. (fill in the blank with such things as "go to a meeting," "do my relaxation exercises," "talk with anyone about this problem," "write in my journal," "pay attention to my life," etc.)

- Drinking, drugging, eating, cutting, etc., is the only answer.
- Everybody else drinks, drugs, binges, cuts, etc.

Have participants identify their own signals that will alert them to the fact that they are at risk of self-sabotaging their own healing. Encourage them to keep a list clearly posted in their homes and to take action to intervene each and every time they occur. Make sure that the participants understand that these thoughts, ideas, feeling, and triggers will occur. If they are prepared for them, they have a greater chance of not sliding back into old self-destructive patterns.

After the Group Ends

■Future Activities to Strengthen Recovery

It is very important for graduates of the ATRIUM groups to engage in activities designed to strengthen recovery. There are no guarantees for success, of course, but there are many types of activities that are helpful. The following areas are organized into subheadings to help group members, group leaders, and other manual users find the right fit for each individual.

Although the activities are subdivided, there are many ways to conceptualize these follow-up ideas for recovery. The graduate may wish to mix activities from each of the categories, and she may think about these activities differently from the way the authors have categorized them. For example, we think of "taking walks and enjoying Nature" as an example of something that belongs under the heading "Enriching the Spirit,"—but someone else could as easily think of this activity as belonging under "Physical Well-being."

The following areas encompass the domains of mind, body, and spirit, and are central to combating the lasting effects of Trauma Reenactment. Not everyone can or will choose to participate in all of the suggested activities, and it is important to emphasize this to the group so that there are no pressures to engage in activities not suited to the person's life circumstances, recovery needs, or personal taste.

Here the areas of follow-through activities are divided into subheadings that seem to have worked best for most people recovering from addiction and trauma who fit the profile of Trauma Reenactment. The five major areas of follow-through activities are: (1) Body-centered Self-care; (2) Spiritual Self-care; (3) Addiction-focused Healing; (4) Trauma-focused Healing; and (5) Social/Environmental Activism.

Body-centered Self-care

The activities in this domain can range from vigorous physical challenges like rope courses, strenuous hiking, and other fitness activities, to basic self-care habits like following a nourishing diet, reducing caffeine intake, and drinking more water. We suggest that ATRIUM graduates be encouraged to choose some activities that are most appropriate and appealing to them, and then discuss with other group members and group leaders how realistic their choices might be.

It is also important to choose activities that are likely to be accessible on a daily or weekly basis. (There are, of course, some occasional events that may be important to include, like a medical check-up, a visit to the dentist, a special kind of once-in-a-while activity like climbing a mountain, or a seasonal activity like planting and caring for a garden.) Generally, setting goals should include activities that can be reasonably achieved. That way, there is less chance of someone giving up after a few failures because she tried an unrealistic type of or amount of the chosen self-care activity.

The following list of body-based self-care activities may give the ATRIUM graduate some ideas so she can choose what best fits her preferences, needs, and life situation.

- Medical self-care: medical check-ups, dental check-ups, informed consumer interactions with medical personnel, medical interventions like necessary surgeries or tests, managing a chronic condition like diabetes
- Basic physical self-care: sleep-improvement practices, healthy eating, drinking more water and less caffeine and/or sugar-saturated products, exercise (daily walks, if possible, stretching, progressive muscle relaxation as part of daily exercise routine), finding more comfortable ways to sit or stand while working and at home
- Alternative health practices: herbal remedies, holistic health awareness and practice, acupuncture, acupressure, chiropractic, Reiki, massage
- Stress reduction practices: mindful breathing, visualization to decrease body tension, progressive muscle relaxation, meditation
- Playing and cultivating self-expression: drumming, chanting, singing, dancing, sports, bike riding, swimming, etc.
- Self-defense training: martial arts and other "street-wise" self-defense skills

Spiritual Self-care

Spiritual self-care is a highly individual choice. By the end of a group, group members and leaders will have a clearer idea of what will fit each individual's various needs, beliefs, preferences, and life circumstances. It is essential for the group to come to a respectful understanding of how ideas about spiritual healing work for each individual and to accept that language, beliefs, and practices may be very different among the group members.

It is equally important not to avoid the subject of spiritual healing in a misguided effort to not offend anyone's sensitivities about spirituality. As the ATRIUM model stresses through the 12 sessions of the group, trauma impacts the spirit as much as the mind and the body, and it is a very significant part of the follow-through activities.

The following list of spiritual self-care activities include a variety of suggestions, but the ATRIUM graduate may have other ideas to fit her beliefs and life situation.

- Meditation: there are many ways to meditate, such as sitting quietly and breathing mindfully, visualizing, and walking meditation; there are also more formal spiritual practices from Buddhism and other "religious" philosophies.
- Prayer: this too is something practiced in many different ways—repeating "I am going to be all right. I am safe and I am loved. I am loved," may be the easiest way to articulate prayer for survivors who are not comfortable with any form of religious-based prayer. The 12-step Serenity Prayer is also recommended.
- Nature-based activities: these activities may include a ritual of spending focused, meditative time with an animal friend or spirit guide; spending time outdoors being mindful of ones connection with the universe; or more extensive outdoor experiences, such as day hiking, outdoor trips, rock climbing, swimming with dolphins, etc.
- Gardening and other outdoor and indoor plant care-taking activities
- 12-step recovery: doing the 12 steps with the guidance of a sponsor is a very important part of healing from addictions and is a highly recommended form of spiritual healing for all Trauma Reenactors.

Addiction-focused Healing

Although the ATRIUM model focuses on recovery from addictions, the 12-week group is certainly not enough by itself to maintain abstinence. In fact, graduates of the ATRIUM model may be at the very beginning of a willingness to enter into the lifelong process of healing and recovery in regard to their addictive behaviors and personality patterns. It is highly recommended that survivors who reenact their traumas through addictions to substances, food, self-injury, alcohol, or relationship patterns, find ways to begin and then maintain a program of abstinence from their addiction. We believe that involvement in 12-step programs is usually the most effective and enduring program for successful recovery.

Recovery from addiction often happens in stages. We recommend:

- Complete immersion in an addiction-focused program, such as a detox facility, a retreat center with strict rules prohibiting use of addictive substances, or a home/community-based program involving 24-hour support for abstinence (where loved ones, volunteers, work colleagues, etc., all commit to supporting the survivor's abstinence from the addictive activity)
- Regular and frequent attendance at 12-step meetings
- Getting a 12-step sponsor
- Working the 12 steps with a sponsor
- Daily practices that support ongoing sobriety from addictive practices, i.e., physical exercise, spiritual supports, community involvement

Trauma-focused Healing

The ATRIUM model graduate has begun to heal from her trauma experience, but she may have more work to do in regard to various aspects of the trauma. There are many excellent models for healing from trauma. The work can take various forms and is, of course, largely determined by what is locally available. The following suggestions are very broad-based rather than specific, but a list of readings in the references may help the TR survivor choose what appeals to her and fits her resources and reading preferences.

- Psychotherapy groups that support women's healing, especially empowerment-based models
- Psychoeducational groups with relevant skill-based components such as DBT, EMDR, relational skill-building, smoking cessation supports, etc.
- Individual counseling or psychotherapy with a focus on relational healing and empowerment
- Bibliotherapy: there are many books about trauma and its impact, but we would caution readers to look for books that focus on resilience and new coping skills rather than readings that emphasize the painful details of individual traumatic experiences. These accounts can be very triggering and create Trauma Reenactment responses that are not helpful in the survivor's recovery process.

Social/Environmental Activism

Like spiritual healing, social activism is a highly individual choice. Traditionally, mental health providers and social services have not included social activism in their approaches to healing and recovery. Yet at least two of the most important influences on the work of healing from addictions and trauma emphasize social activism as central to the healing process: Both Judith Herman's groundbreaking work in the trauma field, *Trauma and Recovery*, and the 12-step program have taught us that people heal best when they can be of service to others.

Each person's healing trajectory is very different. For some survivors of Trauma Reenactment, it may be enough to practice some self-care activities with others, such as going for walks with others from the ATRIUM group or providing peer support via check-ins. For others, being of service via sponsoring or simply supporting others in 12-step recovery may be the appropriate choice of social activism.

Because we understand healing of the spirit as central to recovery from Trauma Reenactment, we also suggest that efforts to protect the natural environment be another form of social activism for ATRIUM graduates. There are many forms of environmental activism, from simply being mindful of protecting local environmental resources to more national or international projects to save whales, trees, wetlands, national parks, etc.

There are many ways to move forward after completing the ATRIUM group. The group, as its name suggests, is an entryway into deeper forms of healing. What is most important is for each survivor of Trauma Reenactment to believe that she is capable of healing, and that she deserves to be healthy, self-accepting, loved, and capable of loving. Whatever path she chooses to follow will be a good path as long as she proceeds in a forward direction. If she finds that she is slipping backwards into repetitive Trauma Reenactment patterns, she is urged to not become stuck in hopelessness or regress to crippling isolation. As the 12-step model so clearly reminds us, recovery is a path of progress, not perfection.

Handouts

■ Session 1

Creating Safety Outside and In:
Purpose of the Group

This 12-week group is designed to help you gain insight and skills in order to better manage the difficult experience of dealing with the effects of trauma and addictions in your life. Traumatic experiences can cause 3-D distress, or distress in the body, the mind, and the spirit. As a result, many people use alcohol, drugs, food, or other forms of addiction to ease their pain. However, these self-destructive behaviors only serve to recreate the self-destruction of early abuse. This group will help you discover ways to stop the self-destructive cycle of Trauma Reenactment.

Group Ground Rules

1. _____
_____
_____
_____

2. _____
_____
_____
_____

3. _____
_____
_____
_____

4. _____
_____
_____
_____

5. _____
_____
_____
_____

6. _____
_____
_____
_____

From *Addictions and Trauma Recovery* © Dusty Miller and Laurie Guidry (W. W. Norton & Company, 2001.)

■ Session 1

"3-D Distress" = Traumatic Stress Response

Fight or Flight Response. *The universal response to threatening and dangerous events.*

Normal Stress→Normal Response. *Under normal conditions, once the threat has passed, the response system returns to homeostasis or balance.*

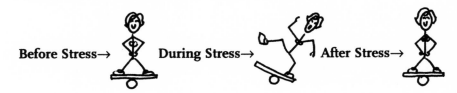

What Goes Wrong. In response to overwhelming stress (such as trauma!), the mechanism which works to help an individual maintain balance (sort of an emotional thermostat or body-mind-spirit regulator) can become dysregulated or function improperly. The "thermostat" can get reset at a high, low, or variable setting. As a result, an individual may try to find other methods to balance the thermostat, such as alcohol, drugs, food, self-harm, etc.

Thermostat too↑!   **Thermostat too↓!**   **Thermostat haywire!**

From *Addictions and Trauma Recovery* © Dusty Miller and Laurie Guidry (W. W. Norton & Company, 2001.)

■ Session 1

Relaxation Response

Practice this 1–2 minutes daily, twice daily to start!

1. Find a *quiet* spot and make yourself *comfortable* in a seated position.

2. Close your eyes or allow your focus to fall gently on the floor a foot or so ahead of you.

3. Breathing in through your nose and out through your mouth, begin to *slow* and *deepen* your breath.

4. As you continue, allow your breath to *fill* your diaphragm—you should be aware of your stomach pressing outward against your clothing. Let the breath *pour* out through your mouth like a vessel pouring water out.

5. Allow your focus to remain on your breath. It is normal for your mind to wander or for you to become distracted. If this happens, each time bring your focus *gently* back to your breath.

6. You may want to focus on a word as you breathe or you may want to count your breath as you inhale and exhale. If you decide to use a word to help you focus, choose a word that brings you *comfort* and *serenity*. If you decide to count, go as high as ten and then start the count over again. You can also choose to focus only on the breath itself.

7. As you breathe, imagine you are breathing in *light* and *energy* and that you are exhaling and *releasing* tension, worry, and discomfort.

8. Do these exercises when you are alert because they help you learn to be relaxed while you are awake. Be patient with yourself as it may take a little time to experience the benefits of this exercise. You can keep track of your progress by noting your experience during the exercise after you have finished.

■ Session 1

Your Experience of 3-D Distress

Body   Mind   Spirit

_____   _____   _____
_____   _____   _____
_____   _____   _____
_____   _____   _____
_____   _____   _____
_____   _____   _____
_____   _____   _____
_____   _____   _____
_____   _____   _____
_____   _____   _____
_____   _____   _____
_____   _____   _____

Notes: _____

_____

_____

■ Session 2

Understanding Trauma Reenactment

What Is Trauma Reenactment?

Trauma Reenactment occurs when trauma and abuse from the past is carried forward into your life today and is reenacted by self-destructive behaviors that either symbolically or literally represent the past trauma.

Then...

Now...

abuse is perpetrated against
the self by others

abuse is perpetrated against
the self by the self

Trauma Reenactment in your life:

Body: _____

_____

_____

_____

_____

Mind: _____

_____

_____

_____

_____

Spirit: _____

_____

_____

_____

_____

From *Addictions and Trauma Recovery* © Dusty Miller and Laurie Guidry (W. W. Norton & Company, 2001.)

What is being reenacted in Trauma Reenactment? The *past abusive relationship* between yourself (Victim), the perpetrator of the trauma (Abuser), and anyone in your life at the time who had the power to stop the abuse but did not (Nonprotecting Bystander).

What is the Triadic Self? The past abusive relationship between yourself (Victim), the perpetrator of the trauma (Abuser), and anyone in your life at the time who had the power to stop the abuse but did not (Nonprotecting Bystander) that is reenacted during trauma reenactment comprises the Triadic Self.

How does this happen? ① Individuals who experience trauma and abuse may *internalize* the 3-way (or triadic) abusive relationship. ② This internalization results in the development of the **Triadic Self** (which includes the **victim-self**, the **abuser-self**, and the **nonprotecting bystander–self**). ③ After taking in the past abusive relationship, the individual then reenacts the dynamics of the early abusive relationship dynamics *over and over again.*

▰Session 2

Messages from and to the Triadic Self

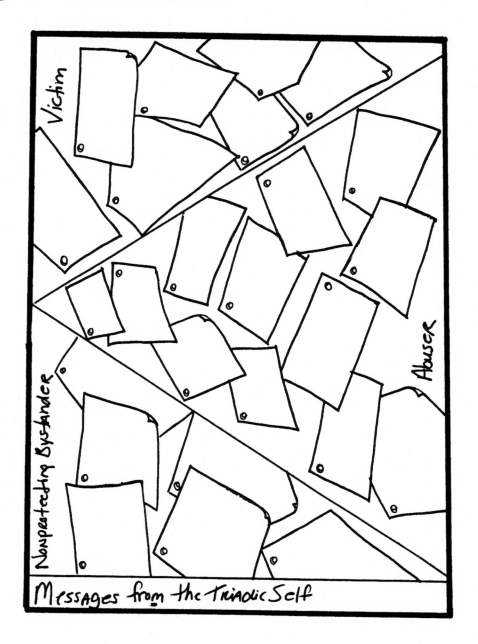

From *Addictions and Trauma Recovery* © Dusty Miller and Laurie Guidry (W. W. Norton & Company, 2001.)

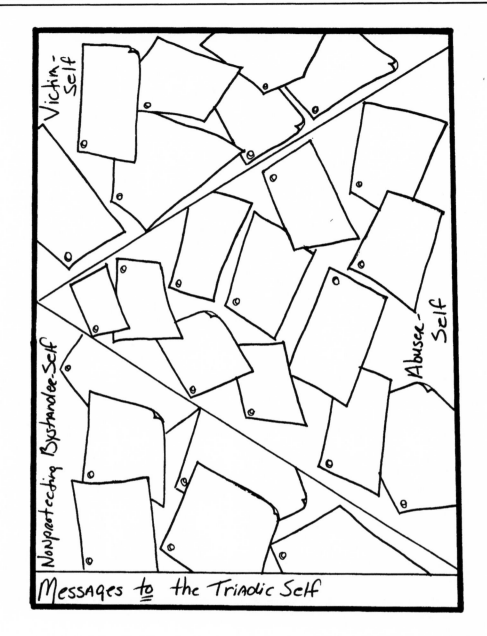

■Session 2

Serenity Prayer

God grant me the serenity
to accept the things I cannot change,
the courage to change the things I can,
and the wisdom to know the difference.

Notes: _____

_____

_____

_____

_____

_____

_____

_____

_____

_____

_____

_____

_____

_____

_____

_____

_____

_____

_____

_____

_____

_____

_____

_____

_____

_____

From *Addictions and Trauma Recovery* © Dusty Miller and Laurie Guidry (W. W. Norton & Company, 2001.)

■Session 3

Addictions and Trauma Reenactment:
Brief Review of Session 2

- *Trauma Reenactment* occurs when trauma and abuse from the past are carried forward into your life today and are reenacted by self-destructive behaviors that either symbolically or literally represent the past trauma.
- *Trauma Reenactment* is an adaptive effort to manage unmanageable 3-D distress.
- *Trauma Reenactment* manifests differently for different people.
- The *Triadic Self* represents the internalization of abusive, nonprotecting, victimizing relationships that occurred during the initial trauma or early abuse.

The Paradox of Addictions and Trauma Reenactment

On one hand, excessive and self-destructive addictions can serve to recreate the experience of early abuse or initial trauma on many different levels. On the other hand, addictions can also serve to provide effective short-term relief from the 3-D distress of trauma.

■Session 3

In what ways might your addiction to drugs, alcohol, food, people, self-injury, etc., be seen/understood/viewed as a reenactment of early abuse or trauma?

Mind:_____
_____
_____
_____
_____
_____
_____
_____
_____

Body:_____
_____
_____
_____
_____
_____
_____
_____
_____
_____

Spirit:_____
_____
_____
_____
_____
_____
_____
_____
_____

◼ Session 3

Cultivating a Protective Presence

What is the **Protective Presence?** The Protective Presence can be thought of as a comforting, soothing, safe, calm resource.

When you hear the word "protective," what words and images come to mind? __

_____
_____
_____
_____
_____
_____
_____
_____
_____
_____
_____
_____
_____

Reflections . . .
What was your experience during the Protective Presence exercise? _____

_____
_____
_____
_____
_____
_____
_____
_____
_____
_____
_____
_____
_____
_____

◼ Session 3

Continuing to Cultivate the Protective Presence in Your Life

Seek to create, hold onto, and make use of lasting sources of safety and comfort in your life. Begin by identifying and writing down current positive sources of support, encouragement, safety, and comfort in your life. This can include everything and anything from pets to poems to music to plants and flowers to your sense of spirituality to specific friends, family, etc. Your resources are your resources! Post this list in a visible area of your home and refer to it often when you are feeling isolated and alone.

Notes: _____

_____
_____
_____
_____
_____
_____
_____
_____
_____
_____
_____
_____
_____
_____
_____
_____
_____
_____
_____
_____
_____
_____
_____
_____

■Session 4

Finding Emotional Expression and Balance: Brief Review of Session 3

The Protective Presence can be thought of as a comforting, soothing, safe, calm resource. *Give examples from your own experience:*_____

_____

_____

_____

_____

_____

_____

_____

_____

The Protective Presence can serve as a replacement for self-destructive efforts at self-soothing like drinking, drugging, eating, etc. *Give examples from your own experience:* _____

_____

_____

_____

_____

_____

_____

_____

_____

_____

The Protective Presence can overcome the Abuser within and the Nonprotecting Bystander within. *Give examples from your own experience:* _____

_____

_____

_____

_____

_____

_____

From *Addictions and Trauma Recovery* © Dusty Miller and Laurie Guidry (W. W. Norton & Company, 2001.)

■ Session 4

How We Lose Our "Emotional Balance" as a Result of Trauma

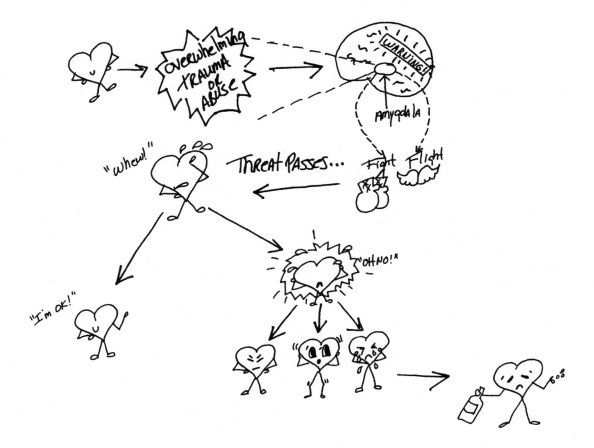

From *Addictions and Trauma Recovery* © Dusty Miller and Laurie Guidry (W. W. Norton & Company, 2001.)

■ Session 4

This Is Important Because . . .

- It is important to understand why trauma can leave us emotionally off-balance because feelings and emotions connect us to ourselves, to others, and to our spirituality. When emotional functioning is disrupted, unpredictable, and unmanageable it is reflected in our lives; our relationship to ourselves, others, and our spirituality becomes disrupted, unpredictable, and unmanageable.
- It is also important to understand that many of the emotions we struggle with in our lives today are **emotional reenactments** of the early abuse or trauma of the past. The undigested or frozen feelings of the Victim (such as fear, despair, confusion, etc.), the Abuser (such as rage, desire for power or control, disgust, etc.), and the Nonprotecting Bystander (apathy, uncertainty, passivity, shame, helplessness, etc.) may play out repeatedly.

Top 5 List of Difficult Emotions:

1. _____
_____
_____
_____

2. _____
_____
_____
_____

3. _____
_____
_____
_____

4. _____
_____
_____
_____

5. _____
_____
_____
_____

■ Session 4

Emotional Balance

In order to try and regain or maintain emotional balance in the past, I have:

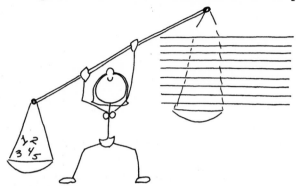

Reflection on Experiential Exercise

What was it like to think about difficult emotions and locate them in your body?

Finding Emotional Balance Through Mindfulness

- When you struggle with difficult feelings, see if you can name them, feel them, and let them go.
- **Naming them** allows you to identify and understand your experience.
- **Feeling them** allows you to validate your experience.
- **Letting them** go allows you to manage unmanageable feelings that can lead to self-destructive behavior.
- Just like the distracting thoughts, images, or tensions that you are aware of in your practice of the relaxation response, when difficult emotions emerge and begin to throw you off-balance, name them, feel them, and let them go!
- And remember, any new skill needs time and practice!

Notes: _____

_____

_____

_____

_____

From *Addictions and Trauma Recovery* © Dusty Miller and Laurie Guidry (W. W. Norton & Company, 2001.)

■ Session 5

Managing Dysregulated Anger:
Whose Anger Is It Anyway?

The anger you feel may not be your own!

Remember this?
Trauma Reenactment

What we are talking about now!
Emotional Reenactment

Specifically:
Toxic Anger

How does toxic anger *show up for you?* _____

_____

_____

_____

_____

_____

_____

_____

■ Session 5

Direction and Control of Anger

Which best describes you when you are in the grip of toxic anger?

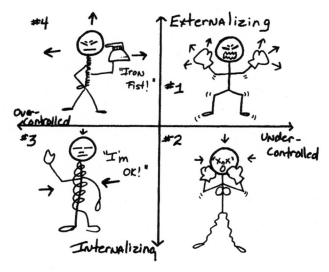

- *Externalizing/Under-Controlled:* acts out against others, short fuse, "hair trigger" temper
- *Internalizing/Under-Controlled:* impulsive, directs rage inward, self-harming
- *Internalizing/Over-Controlled:* "tightly wound," appears in control, anger directed inward, depressed, may have physical problems
- *Externalizing/Over-Controlled:* "control freak," rages against others but in a focused way, "rules with an iron fist" attitude

How do you distinguish healthy anger from toxic anger?

Healthy Anger	Toxic Anger
You can own it.	It is fueled by the Triadic Self.
It is an appropriate fit for the situation.	It is extreme and out of proportion.
It is pointed in the right direction.	It is pointed in the wrong direction.

From *Addictions and Trauma Recovery* © Dusty Miller and Laurie Guidry (W. W. Norton & Company, 2001.)

▬ Session 5

Toxic Anger

What does your anger feel like? _____

_____

_____

_____

What does your anger look like? (draw and/or write below): _____

Who do you direct your anger toward? _____

_____

_____

_____

_____

_____

_____

_____

_____

_____

_____

_____

■ Session 5

Dysregulated Anger

How has your addiction helped you regulate dysreglated anger? _____
_____
_____

*What angers you most about your experience of trauma or abuse?*_____
_____
_____

List positive, healthy expression of anger:

_____   _____
_____   _____
_____   _____
_____   _____

*Reflections on Deep Muscle Relaxation:*_____
_____
_____
_____

Stopping the Locomotion

Whatever the form of your dysregulated anger, do the following to try and manage it in the moment!

1. Stop *before you act.*   3. Think *before you speak.*
2. Name *the feeling before you react.* 4. Release *the tension before you choose.*

In order to better manage your anger, the very first thing you have to do is slow things down! Once you do, you have a better chance of choosing your own course of action rather than being driven by toxic rage! Practice *releasing* tension before you act or speak!

Notes: _____
_____
_____
_____

■ Session 6

Cultivating Courage: Moving beyond Anxiety and Fear

Poll

Have you experienced any of the following phenomena:

___ "spacing out"

___ out-of-body experience

___ difficulty concentrating

___ difficulty sleeping

___ feeling like you are in a dream

___ altered perception of pain

___ altered perception of body

___ fragmented memories

___ emotional numbing

___ separate inner "self"

___ chronic feelings of dread

___ loss of time

___ poor memory

___ daydreaming

___ feeling "unreal"

___ confusion

___ flashbacks

___ tunnel vision

___ nightmares

___ feeling easily startled

___ hypervigilance

___ panic attacks

■ Session 6

Altered Arousal

- *Hyperarousal*, an easily triggered fight or flight reaction
- *Hypervigilance*, a guarded watchfulness due to chronic unsafe feelings, can contribute to difficulties with sleep
- *Exaggerated Startle Response*, when someone is startled and responds out of proportion to the stimulus or trigger
- *Panic Attacks*, which are intense feelings of dread along with increased physiological symptoms like heart palpitations, shortness of breath, shakiness, sweating, tunnel vision, etc.

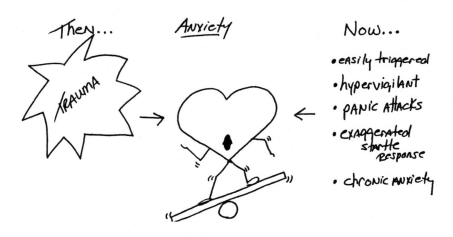

From Addictions and Trauma Recovery © Dusty Miller and Laurie Guidry (W. W. Norton & Company, 2001.)

■Session 6

Altered Consciousness

As hyperarousal increases, one may experience altered states of consciousness. These alterations in consciousness or dissociative phenomena are initially adaptive and occur during the initial trauma to help people continue to function in spite of the threat. However, as the threat continues, there can be a progression from extreme arousal to dissociation.

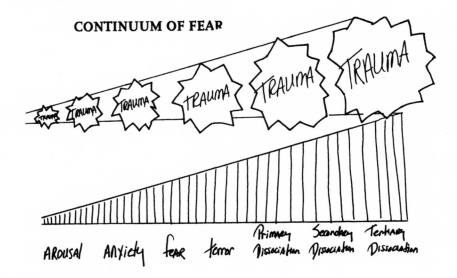

CONTINUUM OF FEAR

AROUSAL   ANXIETY   FEAR   terror   Primary Dissociation   Secondary Dissociation   Tertiary Dissociation

Dissociation of the Mind

Primary Dissociation is the first level of dissociation and entails a splitting off of **cognition** from consciousness in the face of extreme threat. This is reflected in individual experience as over- or under-integration of the traumatic event. This type of recall can lead to intrusive recollections, flashbacks, and nightmares and can lead to PTSD.

■Session 6

Dissociation of the Body

Secondary dissociation involves the splitting off of **affect** or emotion from consciousness in the face of an extreme danger or threat to personal integrity. This is also referred to as peritraumatic dissociation and can include out-of-body experiences (i.e., watching the event happen as if from a distance); altered or distorted experiences of time, place, or person; feeling "unreal;" confusion; bewilderment; changes in capacity for pain perception; alterations in body image; and tunnel vision.

Dissociation of the Spirit

Tertiary dissociation is the most extreme form of dissociative phenomenon. It involves a complete split from consciousness and the development of a different ego state to contain the trauma. This can sometimes lead to dissociative disorders.

Some level of dissociation during a stressful and traumatic experience occurs to most people. It is what happens in the aftermath that can become most problematic for survivors of trauma and abuse.

■ Session 6

Finding Courage

How have you carried a legacy of fear with you since your own experience of trauma or abuse? _____

_____

_____

_____

_____

How have you used your addiction to calm your fears and reduce your anxiety? _____

_____

_____

_____

_____

Alcohol is often referred to as "courage in a bottle." In what more positive ways have you sought **courage** *in your life?* _____

_____

_____

_____

_____

What are you now most afraid of or anxious about? _____

_____

_____

_____

_____

How might you now deal with these fears and worries differently? _____

_____

_____

_____

_____

_____

From *Addictions and Trauma Recovery* © Dusty Miller and Laurie Guidry (W. W. Norton & Company, 2001.)

▦ Session 6

Travel Log

On your journey to your safe place,
where did you go? _____

_____

_____

_____

what did you see? _____

_____

_____

what did you smell? _____

_____

_____

what did you taste? _____

_____

_____

what did you feel? _____

_____

_____

what did you think? _____

_____

_____

Other important details: _____

_____

_____

_____

Remember: You can go to this safe place any time **you choose to!**

■ Session 6

Cultivating Courage

- What does courage mean to you?
- In what ways are you a courageous person?
- Make a list of the courageous things you do on a daily basis:

_____ _____
_____ _____
_____ _____
_____ _____
_____ _____
_____ _____
_____ _____
_____ _____
_____ _____
_____ _____
_____ _____

Notes: _____

_____

_____

_____

_____

_____

_____

_____

_____

_____

_____

_____

■ Session 7

The Body Remembers What the Spirit Seeks to Forget

*Reflections on the body scan exercise:*_____

_____

_____

_____

_____

_____

_____

_____

_____

_____

_____

_____

_____

_____

_____

True/False Quiz

1. Memory is located in the brain.   T   F
2. During traumatic experiences, the part of the brain
   associated with speech and language decreases in
   activity while the part of the brain that is associated
   with emotion increases in activity.   T   F
3. During trauma, memory may become "hard-wired"
   (or imprinted strongly) in your memory.   T   F
4. Suppressing negative emotions can lead to impaired
   immune system functioning and illnesses.   T   F
5. Your pain and illness is all in your head.   T   F
6. The mind-body connection is a highly complex
   and interrelated relationship—what affects the mind
   also affects the body.   T   F
7. Your pain and illness are **real**!   T   F

From *Addictions and Trauma Recovery* © Dusty Miller and Laurie Guidry (W. W. Norton & Company, 2001.)

■ Session 7

Do You Remember . . .

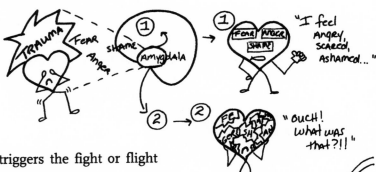

Overwhelming trauma triggers the fight or flight response.

↓

Perceptions of the trauma then take a shortcut, bypassing the part of the brain that evaluates, processes, labels, categorizes, and integrates perceptions and experiences into memory in a way that makes sense.

↓

Because this process gets bypassed, emotions linked with overwhelming, traumatic experiences may not be fully processed.

↓

New information . . .

↓

As a result, unprocessed, unnamed emotions can be experienced as physical sensations in the body. (sort of like "unidentifiable body emotions")

↓

These body emotions can get activated by memories of the initial trauma, stress, or fatigue; the onset of emotions is similar to those experienced during the initial trauma. (sort of like "body reenactment")

↓

Chronic activation of these nameless emotions in the body can potentially lead to physical discomfort, a disruption of systemic functioning, and illnesses.

■ Session 7

What Do You Think . . .

What have been the dominant messages or most common responses and reactions that you have received from others when you have been sick or in physical pain? _____

_____

_____

_____

_____

_____

_____

What reactions or responses would have been more helpful to you at the time?

_____

_____

_____

_____

_____

_____

_____

Where do you think you carry the pain of your trauma experience in your body? _____

_____

_____

_____

_____

_____

_____

What experiences have made your body stronger and more resilient?

_____

_____

_____

_____

_____

_____

_____

■ **Session 7**

Journaling as a Step toward Healing
the Body-Mind-Spirit

Writing about negative experiences helps improve health and well-being. Journaling has many positive benefits in the healing process and is an important factor in maintaining change and in monitoring the ongoing healing process in one's life. List below some of the positive benefits of journaling. If you have not included journaling in your healing process as of yet, begin today!

Benefits of Journaling

_____

_____

_____

_____

_____

_____

_____

_____

_____

_____

_____

Notes: _____

_____

_____

_____

_____

_____

_____

_____

_____

_____

_____

From *Addictions and Trauma Recovery* © Dusty Miller and Laurie Guidry (W. W. Norton & Company, 2001.)

■Session 8

Your Body Is a Gift

Reflections on the introductory exercise—tuning into the body

_____

_____

_____

Looking Through the Distorted Lens of the Triadic Self

Experiences of trauma and abuse often distort a survivor's body image. Individuals may take negative actions because of these inaccurate ideas about their bodies. What ideas do you have about your body as a result of your trauma?

_____

_____

_____

Have these ideas influenced you to take negative actions against your body? If so, what were they?

_____

_____

_____

_____

Key Points to Remember

- Body image can become distorted by experiences of trauma or abuse.
- As a result, survivors often view their bodies through the distorted lens of the Triadic Self.
- Survivors may view and treat their bodies in abusive, nonprotecting, and victimizing ways.
- The distortions you hold about your body are lies told to you by the Triadic Self. It is time to gently take off the distorted lens you have worn for so long and slowly begin to see your body as the "gift" it really is!!!

■ Session 8

Changing Lens ✍

Question 1: What is your favorite body part and why? _____

_____
_____
_____
_____
_____
_____

Question 2: What is the strongest part of your body and why? _____

_____
_____
_____
_____
_____
_____

Question 3: What is a special thing your body can do? _____

_____
_____
_____
_____
_____
_____

Question 4: Name at least three positive, nurturing things your body likes best.

_____
_____
_____
_____
_____
_____

■Session 8

Your Body Is a Gift

List all the items you placed in your "gift box":

_____

_____

_____

_____

_____

_____

Record the message on your card: _____

_____

_____

_____

_____

_____

Make a list of self-care issues you would like to attend to over time:

_____ _____

_____ _____

_____ _____

_____ _____

_____ _____

Notes: _____

_____

_____

_____

_____

_____

_____

Remember: Your body is a vessel for your spirit. Tend the vessel and the spirit flourishes.

◼️Session 9

Touch and Intimacy

Brief review of trauma reenactment and the triadic self:

- *Trauma Reenactment* occurs when trauma and abuse from the past is carried forward into your life today and is reenacted by self-destructive behaviors that either symbolically or literally represent past trauma.
- *Trauma Reenactment* is an adaptive effort to manage unmanageable 3-D distress.
- *Trauma Reenactment* manifests differently for different people.
- *The Triadic Self* represents the internalization of abusive, nonprotecting, victimizing relationships that occur during the initial trauma or early abuse.

Remember the "paradox" of addictions and Trauma Reenactment?

The same can be true of sex and Trauma Reenactment!

From *Addictions and Trauma Recovery* © Dusty Miller and Laurie Guidry (W. W. Norton & Company, 2001.)

■Session 9

Touch and Intimacy

On one hand, excessive and self-destructive addiction—such as distressing sexual activities and situations—can serve to recreate the experience of early abuse or initial trauma on many different levels. On the other hand, these situations can also serve to provide effective short-term relief from the 3-D distress of trauma.

In what ways might your experiences with touch, physical closeness, sexual activities, and fantasies be seen/understood/viewed as reenactments of early abuse or trauma?

Mind:_____

_____

_____

_____

_____

_____

Body: _____

_____

_____

_____

_____

_____

Spirit:_____

_____

_____

_____

_____

_____

From *Addictions and Trauma Recovery* © Dusty Miller and Laurie Guidry (W. W. Norton & Company, 2001.)

▄ Session 9

Cultivating a Protective Presence

What is the **Protective Presence?**
The Protective Presence can be a comforting, soothing, safe, calm resource.

When you hear the word "protective," what words and images come to mind? __

_____
_____
_____
_____
_____
_____
_____
_____
_____
_____

Reflections . . .
What was your experience during the Protective Presence exercise?

_____
_____
_____
_____
_____
_____
_____
_____
_____
_____
_____

From *Addictions and Trauma Recovery* © Dusty Miller and Laurie Guidry (W. W. Norton & Company, 2001.)

■Session 9

Cultivating the Protective Presence in Your Life

In order to combat the negative messages we carry around inside us about touch, sexuality, and physical closeness, we need to create and make use of lasting sources of safety and comfort. This week, continue to identify (and write down) current positive sources of support, encouragement, comfort, and acceptance in your life. This can include everything and anything from pets to poems to music to plants and flowers to your sense of spirituality to specific friends and family. You are the expert in creating your own Protective Presence.

Words may not be enough to describe your Protective Presence. You can also create images through drawings, collages, pictures, or favorite music. If you feel comfortable doing so, post your images and your list in a visible area of your room and refer to it often when you are feeling isolated and alone. If you have music to remind you of your Protective Presence, remember to listen to it whenever you have a few minutes.

Notes: _____

_____

_____

_____

_____

_____

_____

_____

_____

_____

_____

_____

_____

_____

_____

_____

_____

_____

■ Session 10

From Reenactment to Reconnection

Reflections on the "Mirror, Mirror . . ." exercise:

_____
_____
_____
_____
_____
_____

Myths about relationships and connection:

Myth #1: _____

Myth #2: _____

Myth #3: _____

Myth #4: _____

Myth #5: _____

Points to Remember

- The most painful wound suffered as a result of trauma or abuse is often the wound of disconnection.
- A traumatic relationship can create a powerful and distorted imprint that can influence how one understands what relationships are and what they mean as well as affect one's ability to connect with others in healthy ways.
- Relational reenactment can occur when negative, abusive, and destructive relational models from the past influence and guide an individual's current relational patterns.
- Alcohol and drugs can be substitutes for relationships with others, ease social discomfort, and bring a false sense of connection or facilitate the self-destructive cycle of relational reenactment.
- We can move from relational reenactment to relational reconnection by creating healing connections with others!

■ Session 10

Questions to explore and reflect upon:

What are your biggest barriers to or fears of connection? _____

_____

_____

_____

_____

_____

How is your addiction like a relationship? _____

_____

_____

_____

_____

_____

How have you used your addiction to manage disconnection? _____

_____

_____

_____

_____

_____

How have you been able to connect with others despite your experience of relational wounding? _____

_____

_____

_____

_____

_____

Name some ways you can overcome your barriers to connection. _____

_____

_____

_____

_____

_____

■ Session 10

Challenge Your Myths!

Challenge to Myth #1: _____

_____

_____

_____

_____

Challenge to Myth #2: _____

_____

_____

_____

_____

Challenge to Myth #3: _____

_____

_____

_____

_____

Challenge to Myth #4: _____

_____

_____

_____

_____

Challenge to Myth #5: _____

_____

_____

_____

_____

■Session 10

Reconnecting with the Self: Reconnecting Your Spirit

Step 1. List all the qualities that you admire and value in someone you would want to have a connection with:

_____   _____
_____   _____
_____   _____
_____   _____
_____   _____

Step 2. Now add *self* in front of each of these.

Self- _____   Self- _____
Self- _____   Self- _____
Self- _____   Self- _____

Step 3. Over time, and with intention, begin to cultivate these qualities within yourself.

Notes: _____
_____
_____
_____
_____
_____
_____
_____
_____
_____
_____
_____
_____

If you want self-esteem, do "esteemable" things!

■ Session 11

Environmental Healing: Spirit in Community

- Healing the spirit is as important as healing the body and mind.
- The ATRIUM model views spiritual distress as a breakdown in connection with the larger community, as well as a feeling of pervasive despair, an unwillingness to trust, and a breakdown of faith.
- "Spirit" may mean fellowship, love, friendship, or a relationship with God, Goddess, a Higher Power, or Nature. However it is described, it is a process through which healing equals renewed hope by reconnecting with a supportive community, the continued strengthening of the Protective Presence, and a deeper sense of trust and comfort in one's relationship with Nature.

This week we encourage you to make healing connections with each other; with nonhuman sources of support in Nature such as pets, plants, trees, water, and birds; and with your "safe space" by bringing the outdoors into the visualization exercise.

Keep notes on how your connection with Nature, other group members, and your safe space impacts your 3-D distress levels. Use words or a scale from 1–5 where 1=doesn't help at all and 5=this *really* helps.

When I connected with another group member, it impacted my 3-D distress as follows:

Mind   *Body*   *Spirit*

When I connected with _____ (nonhuman form of support), it impacted my 3-D distress as follows:

Mind   *Body*   *Spirit*

When I visualized my safe space, it impacted my 3-D distress as follows:

Mind   *Body*   *Spirit*

■ Session 11

Continuing to Cultivate the Protective Presence

Remember that the Protective Presence can be thought of as a comforting, soothing, safe, calm resource—an important deepening of your spiritual well-being.

When you hear the words "Protective Presence" now, what words and images come to mind? _____

_____

Reflections . . .
What was your experience during the "going outdoors" exercise? _____

_____

_____

_____

What was your experience during the "creating a safe space" exercise? What idea or images did you bring from your outdoors experience into your safe space? ___

_____

_____

_____

_____

You are the expert in creating your own Protective Presence. Remember that words may not be enough to describe your Protective Presence. You can also create images through drawings, collages, pictures, or favorite music. If you have music to remind you of your Protective Presence, remember to listen to it whenever you can take a few minutes.

You can also find your Protective Presence by going outdoors or visualizing a healing outside environment where you would like to be. Refer to it often when you are feeling isolated or alone.

Notes: _____

_____

_____

■**Session 12**

The Journey toward Hope

Notes on Session Review: _____

_____

_____

List of Significant Insights

_____

_____

_____

_____

_____

List of Changes Made

_____

_____

_____

_____

_____

What Was Most Helpful

_____

_____

_____

_____

_____

What Was Most Difficult

_____

_____

_____

_____

_____

Favorite Part of Group

_____

_____

_____

_____

_____

Least Favorite Part of Group

_____

_____

_____

_____

_____

What was the one thing you wish someone had told you prior to the start of group? _____

_____

_____

_____

■Session 12

Warning Signs!

Identify risky thoughts, behaviors, feelings, and triggers (which can be people, places, things) that can signal you that you are at risk of falling back into self-destructive patterns on the lefthand side of the table. Describe on the right how you will intervene. The first three lines provide examples.

Warning Signs	New Response
"One drink won't hurt"	Challenge the thought
Feeling depressed and isolating	Reach out to friends
"I'm worthless"	"That's the Abuser talking. It's a lie!"

From *Addictions and Trauma Recovery* © Dusty Miller and Laurie Guidry (W. W. Norton & Company, 2001.)

▄▄Session 12

Reflections on Final Group

_____
_____
_____
_____
_____
_____
_____
_____
_____
_____
_____
_____
_____
_____
_____
_____
_____
_____
_____
_____
_____
_____
_____
_____
_____
_____
_____
_____
_____
_____
_____
_____

References

Albach, F., & Everaerd, W. (1992). Post traumatic stress symptoms in victims of childhood incest. *Psychotherapeutic Psychometrics, 57*(4): 143–151.

Alexander M. J., & Muenzenmaier, K. (1998). Trauma, addiction and recovery: Addressing public health epidemics among women with severe mental illness. In B. Levin, A. Blanch, and A. Jennings (Eds.), *Women's mental health services: A public health perspective.* Thousand Oaks, CA: Sage.

American Medical Association (AMA). (1992). Violence against women: Relevance for medical practitioners. *Journal of the American Medical Association, 267*(23), 3184–3189.

Barrett, M. J. (1999). Healing from trauma. In F. Walsh (Ed.), *Spirituality resources in family therapy* (pp. 193–208). New York: Guilford.

Brayden, R. M. (1995). Evidence for specific effects of childhood sexual abuse on mental well-being and physical self-esteem. *The International Journal of Child Abuse and Neglect, 19*(10): 1255–1262.

Briere, J. R. (1988). Long-term clinical correlates of childhood sexual victimization. Human sexual aggression: Current perspectives. *Annals of the New York Academy of Sciences, 528:* 327–334.

Briere, J. R., & Runtz, M. (1988). Multivariate correlates of childhood psychological and physical maltreatment among university women. *Childhood Abuse and Neglect, 12:* 331–341.

Briere, J., & Zaidi, L. Y. (1989). Sexual abuse histories and sequelae in female psychiatric emergency room patients. *American Journal of Psychiatry, 146*(12): 1603-1606.

Browne, A., & Bassuk, S. (1997). Intimate violence in the lives of homeless and poor housed women: Prevalence and patterns in an ethnically diverse sample. *American Journal of Orthopsychiatry, 67*:261–278.

Browne, A., & Finkelhor, D. (1986). Impact of child sexual abuse: A review of the research. *Psychological Bulletin, 99*, 66–77.

Brown, V. B., Huba, G. J., & Melchlor, L. A. (1995). Level of burden: Women with more than one co-occurring disorder. *Journal of Psychoactive Drugs, 27*(4): 339–346.

Carmen, E. H. (1995). Inner city community mental health: The interplay of abuse and race in chronic mentally ill women. In C. V Willie, P. P. Rieker, B. M. Kramer, & B. S. Brown (Eds.), *Mental health: Racism and sexism* (pp. 217–236). Pittsburgh: Pittsburgh University Press.

Canon, W. B. (1932). *The wisdom of the body.* New York: Plenum Press.

Conterio, K., and Lader, W. (1998). *Bodily harm.* New York: Hyperion.

Dallam, S. J. (1997). The identification and management of self-mutilating patients in primary care. *The Nurse Practitioner, 22*(5): 151–153, 159–165.

Diamond, D. (2000). *Sober means to narrative ends.* Oakland, CA: Guilford.

Doob, D. (1992). Female sexual abuse survivors as patients: Avoiding retraumatization. *Archives of Psychiatric Nursing, 6*(4): 245–251.

Dreshman-Chiodo, J. (1997). Psychospiritual transformation and the healing process: An assessment of well-being, critical life events, and trauma in relation to spiritual groups. *Dissertation Abstracts International, 57*(10-A): 4416. (From PsycINFO, accession number 1997-95007-034).

Drossman, D., Leserman, J., Nachman, G., Li, A., Gluck, H., Toomey, T., & Mitchell, C. (1990). Sexual and physical abuse among women with functional and organic gastrointestinal disorders. *Annals of Internal Medicine, 113*, 828–833.

Federal Bureau of Investigation. (1992). *Uniform crime statistics.* Washington, DC: Government Printing Office.

Glover, N. M., Janikowski, T. P., & Benshoff, J. J. (1996). Substance abuse and past incest contact: A national perspective. *Journal of Substance Abuse Treatment, 13*(3): 185–193.

Green, B. L., Epstein, S. A., Krupnick, J. L., & Rowland, J. H. (1997). Trauma and medical illness: Assessing trauma-related disorders in medical settings. In J. P. Wilson and T. M. Keane (Eds.), *Assessing psychological trauma and PTSD* (pp. 160–191). New York: Guilford.

Harris, M. (1994). Modifications in service delivery and clinical treatment for women diagnosed with severe mental illness who are also the survivors of sexual abuse trauma. *Journal of Mental Health Administration, 21*: 397–406.

Harris, M., & The Community Connections Trauma Work Group. (1998). *Trauma recovery and empowerment: A clinician's guide to working with women in groups.* New York: Free Press.

Haswell, D. E., & Graham, M. (1996). Self-inflicted injuries: Challenging knowledge, skills and compassion. *Canadian Family Physician, 42:* 1756–1758, 1761–1764.

Herman, J. L. (1992a). Complex PTSD: A syndrome in survivors of prolonged and repeated trauma. *Journal of Traumatic Stress, 5:* 377–391.

Herman, J. L. (1992b). *Trauma and recovery: The aftermath of violence from domestic abuse to political terror.* New York: Basic.

Herman, J. L., Perry, J. C., & van der Kolk, B. A. (1985). Childhood trauma in borderline personality disorder. *American Journal of Psychiatry, 146,* 146–149.

Janes, J. (1994). Their own worst enemy? Management and prevention of self-harm. *Professional Nursing, 9(12):* 838–841.

Jennings, A. (1997). On being invisible in the mental health system. In M. Harris & C. Landis (Eds.), *Sexual abuse in the lives of women diagnosed with serious mental illness* (pp. 162–180). Netherlands: Harwood Academic.

Krystal, H. (1988). *Integration and self-healing: Affect, trauma, and alexithymia.* Hillsdale, NJ: Analytic Press.

Landecker, H. (1992). The role of childhood sexual trauma in the etiology of borderline personality disorder: Considerations for diagnosis and treatment. *Psychotherapy, 29:* 234–242.

Lechner, M. E., Vogel, M. E., Garcia-Shelton, L. M., Leichter, J. L., & Steibel, K. R. (1993). Self-reported medical problems of adult female survivors of childhood sexual abuse. *Journal of Family Practice, 36(6):* 633.

Leserman, J., Drossman, D. A., Li, Z., Toomey, T. C., Nachman, G., & Glocau, L. (1996). Sexual and physical abuse history in gastroenterology practice: How types of abuse impact health status. *Psychosomatic Medicine, 58:* 4–15.

Linehan, M. (1993a). *Cognitive-behavioral treatment of borderline personality disorder.* New York: Guilford.

Linehan, M. (1993b). *Skills training manual for treating borderline personality disorder.* New York: Guilford.

Manley, J. O. (1999). Battered women and their children: A public policy response. *Affilia, 14(4):* 439–459.

Miller, D. (1990). Women in pain: Substance abuse/self-medication. In M. Mirkin (Ed.), *Social and political contexts of family therapy* (pp. 179–192). New York: Gardner.

Miller, D. (1991). Are we keeping up with Oprah? In C. Bepko (Ed.), *Feminism and addiction* (pp. 103–126). New York: Haworth.

Miller, D. (1992). Incest: The heart of darkness. In E. Imber-Black (Ed.), *Secrets in families and family therapy* (pp. 181–195). New York: Norton.

Miller, D. (1994). *Women who hurt themselves: A book of hope and understanding.* New York: Basic.

Miller, D. (1996). Challenging self-harm through transformation of the trauma story. *Sexual Addiction and Compulsivity, 3(3):* 213–227.

Miller, D., Guidry, L., & Daly, H. (1999, April). *Treating trauma within the mind/body context*. Invited symposium at the Annual Meeting of the Eastern Psychological Association, Boston, MA.

Mirowski, J., & Ross, C. E. (1995). *Social causes of psychological distress*. New York: Aldine de Gruyter.

Moeller, T. P., Bachmann, G. A., & Moeller, J. R. (1993). The combined effects of physical, sexual and emotional abuse during childhood: Long-term health consequences for women. *Child Abuse & Neglect, 17*: 623–640.

Muenzenmaier, K., Meyer, I., Struening, E., & Ferber, J. (1993). Childhood abuse and neglect among women outpatients with chronic mental illness. *Hospital and Community Psychiatry, 44*: 666–670.

Najavits, L. M., Weiss, R. D., & Liese, B. S. (1996). Group cognitive behavioral therapy for women with PTSD and substance use disorder. *Journal of Substance Abuse Treatment, 13*(1): 13–22.

Najavits, L. M., Weiss, R. D., Shaw, S. R., & Muenz, L. R. (1998). "Seeking safety": Outcome of a new cognitive-behavioral psychotherapy for women with post-traumatic stress disorder and substance dependence. *Journal of Traumatic Stress, 11*(3): 437–456.

Pearlman, L., & Saakvitne, K. (1995). *Trauma and the therapist*. New York: Norton.

Pittman, R. K., van der Kolk, B. A., Orr, S. P., & Greenberg, M. S. (1990). Naloxene-reversible analgesic response to combat-related stimuli in posttraumatic stress disorder. *Archives of General Psychiatry, 47*: 541–544.

Policy Research, Inc. (1994). *Practical approaches in the treatment of women who abuse alcohol and other drugs*. DHHS Pub. No. (SMA) 94-3006. Rockville, MD: Center for Substance Abuse Treatment.

Prescott, L. (1998). *Women emerging in the wake of violence*. Culver City, CA: Prototypes Systems Change Center.

Pribor. E. F., Yutzy, S. H., Dean, J. T., & Wetzel, R. D. (1993). Briquet's syndrome, dissociation and abuse. *Journal of American Psychiatry, 149*: 52–56.

Roberts, A. (1998). *Battered women and their families: Intervention strategies and treatment programs*. New York: Springer.

Rose, S., Peabody, C. G., & Stratigeas, B. (1991). Undetected abuse among intensive case management clients. *Hospital and Community Psychiatry, 42*(5), 499–503.

Saakvitne, K., Gamble, S., Pearlman, L., & Lev, B. (2000). *Risking connection*. Joppa, MD: Sidran.

Salasin, S. E. (1986). Introduction: A blow of redirection. In S. Neiderbach (Ed.), *Invisible wounds: Crime victims speak* (pp. 1–3). New York: Hayworth.

Schnurr, P.P. (1996). Trauma, PTSD, and physical health. *PTSD Research Quarterly, 7*(3): 213–227.

Shapiro, F. (1995). *Eye movement desensitization and reprocessing.* New York: Guilford.

Shapiro, S., & Dominiak, G. (1992). *Sexual trauma and psychopathology.* New York: Macmillan.

van der Kolk, B. A. (1996). The complexity of adaptation to trauma: Self-regulation, stimulus discrimination, and characterological development. In B. A. van der Kolk, A. C. McFarlane, & L. Weiseth (Eds.), *Traumatic stress: The effects of overwhelming experience on mind and body, and society* (pp. 182–213). New York: Guilford.

van der Kolk, B. A., McFarlane, A. C., & Weiseth, L. (1996). *Traumatic stress: The effects of overwhelming experience on mind and body, and society.* New York: Guilford.

van der Kolk, B. A., van der Hart, O., & Marmar, C. R. (1996). Dissociation and information processing in posttraumatic stress disorder. In B. A. van der Kolk, A. C. McFarlane, & L. Weiseth (Eds.), *Traumatic stress: The effects of overwhelming experience on mind, body, and society* (pp. 303–327). New York: Guilford.

Walker, E. A., Gelfand, A., Katon, W. J., Koss, M. P., Von Korff, M., Bernstein, D., & Russo, J. (1999). Adult health status of women with histories of childhood abuse and neglect. *American Journal of Medicine, 107*: 332–339.

Walker, E. A., Katon, W. J., Roy-Byrne, P. P., Jemelka, R. P., & Russo, J. (1993). Histories of sexual victimization in patients with irritable bowel syndrome or inflammatory bowel disease. *American Journal of Psychiatry, 150*(10), 1502–1506.

Warshaw, C. (1995). Violence and women's health: Old models, new challenges. In *Dare to vision: Shaping the national agenda for women, abuse and mental health services. Proceedings of a conference held July 14–16, 1994 in Arlington, VA, co-sponsored by the Center for Mental Health Services and Human Association of the Northeast* (pp. 67–85). Holyoke, MA: Human Resource Association.

Young, L. (1992). Sexual abuse and the problem of embodiment. *Journal of Child Abuse and Neglect, 16*: 89–100.

Zlotnick, C., Shea, M. T., Recupero, P., Bidadi, K., Pearlstein, T., & Brown, P. (1997). Trauma, dissociation, impulsivity, and self-mutilation among substance abuse patients. *American Journal of Orthopsychiatry, 67*(4): 650–654.

Index